Ian McEwan was born in England in 1948 and began writing in 1970. In 1976 he received the Somerset Maugham Award for his collection of short stories, *First Love, Last Rites*. This was followed by another collection, *In Between the Sheets*. His previous novels are *The Cement Garden* and *The Comfort of Strangers*, which were shortlisted for the 1981 Booker McConnell Prize. *The Child in Time* won the Whitbread Prize for fiction in 1987. All these titles are published in Picador, together with *The Imitation Game*, a collection of three plays for television.

Also by Ian McEwan in Picador

Ian McEwan

A MOVE ABROAD:
or Shall We Die? *and*
The Ploughman's Lunch

published by Pan Books

or *Shall We Die?* first published 1983 by Jonathan Cape Ltd
© Ian McEwan 1983

The Ploughman's Lunch first published 1985 by Methuen
Copyright in the screenplay © Ian McEwan 1985
The fragment of poem in Scene 32 is by Christopher Reid

Note: or *Shall We Die?* was commissioned from Ian McEwan and Michael
Berkeley by the London Symphony Orchestra Chorus with funds
provided by the Arts Council of Great Britain. It was first
performed at the Royal Festival Hall on 6 February 1983 by
Heather Harper (Soprano) and Stephen Roberts (Baritone) and
the London Symphony Orchestra and Chorus conducted by Richard Hickox.
or *Shall We Die?* is available on EMI record and disc. Performance details
as above but with David Wilson-Johnson as baritone.
Record: ASD 270058'
Disc: CDM 7 69810 2

This Picador edition first published 1989 by
Pan books, Cavaye Place, London SW10 9PG

9 8 7 6 5 4 3 2 1

ISBN 0 330 30940 4

Phototypeset by Input Typesetting Ltd, London
Printed in Great Britain by Richard Clay Ltd, Bungay, Suffolk

Contents

Preface

These two very different pieces of writing belong together.
They were written in response to particular situations at the
beginning of this decade. They represent flights from, or
tactical evasions of, novel writing, and as such they taught
me something about the relationship between ideas, opinions,
politics, bees-in-the-bonnet on the one hand and the
imagination on the other. Taken together, these two pieces
were the groundwork for the novel I began in 1983, *The
Child in Time*. I have always wanted to put them together in
a book, and since their decade is almost over and the matters
they addressed are still with us, this seems the moment to do
it.

What is it, to be thinking of a novel you might write? You
put your feet up on the radiator, tilt back your chair and
looking unseeingly out the window. In a state that is both
passive and alert, you allow the fragments to return. It could
be a sequence of events, less than that, a situation: a man is
standing by the side of a busy road with two heavy suitcases.
They contain the dissected body of his lover's ex-husband. He
knows he ought to take them to the station. The plan was
to deposit them in the left luggage lockers. But he wants to
go home first, he needs to think, he needs to sit down. He
needs a sleep, just twenty minutes. And the cases are so
heavy. Can he risk a taxi? Does he have the money? Perhaps
it is a time, a time when much was made of the cigarette in

the methods of seduction, and when a young, naïve
Englishman would have learned how to cup his hand, light
his, light hers, toss the match, whatever, at his local cinema.
And there is a city, Moscow, no, too difficult to know,
Vienna perhaps, Berlin. Then it is this man again, a version
of yourself, but ferociously organized, meticulous,
manipulable and socially inept, someone you might have
become if your luck had been really atrocious. Now it's his
work that draws you, something technical. Electronics in its
earliest days, there is something indefinably attractive about
that. There is his American friend who is also his boss,
bullying but friendly, always touching our man, pulling on
his lapel to make a point, guiding him by the elbow to a quiet
part of the room. And there is a tunnel being dug, in secret.
You dug tunnels as a child, dangerously unsupported burrows
thirty feet long. The smell of damp earth, the special quality
of silence, the panic you had to control when you were down
there. Kafka's paranoid burrower, not his best story, but the
one you remember best . . .

This could be the tenth time in a week that these pieces have
jostled before you. If you wake in the night, they are
instantly there. The fragments belong, but you do not yet
know how. There is something self-evident here, you are
being offered something, there is an urgency you cannot
ignore, you better not fall asleep. Turn on the light, *there is
something in this for you*.

And without giving a second thought, you know that you do
not need to ask what it means, what the *idea* is, or stands
for, or what you will intend, or what designs you have on an
imaginary reader. That will look after itself. It looks like you
are choosing this, and you will simply have to trust your taste,
your inclinations. You have no influence with the real world,
you no longer give a damn about the real world, whatever

that is. For now, the world is these details, the relation between them, the echoes whose urgency is their only justification, the character like someone half-remembered and now drifting into focus, the city you might have to revisit.

And beyond the pieces, is the prospect of making a shape, a form that is self-sustaining, self-justifying and balanced in terms which you cannot quite define or prescribe; you will know it when you see it. You will know when you are satisfied. All this is making you excited and miserable. You have got something, but do you have the energy, the patience, the talent, to find out what it really is, can you do it justice? Which are the inessential fragments? Perhaps you should start today, and by writing discover more. Perhaps you need more time by the radiator.

This hypothetical beginning, this particular sweat, is what I take to be imaginative freedom. Of course, novels can present themselves initially in a far less elusive manner. They can arrive virtually intact. You could map one out, paragraph by paragraph. But even with the most rigorous of schemes at your elbow, the best writing, the real discoveries and almost certainly the greatest pleasures will come from precisely what is unplanned. To be surprised in the act of creation! Why else put up with the drudgery and loneliness? There is a degree of self-pleasuring about imaginative writing which has not been remotely assimilated by literary theory, nor would it make any difference if it had.

It is this necessity of pleasurable surprise in the moment of writing that is so difficult to reconcile with hard ideas, social theories, axes-to-grind, persuasive intentions or the determination to be right. Milan Kundera, who by the standards of English writers is a vigorous metaphysician of his art, is a dependable guide on this: 'The novelist makes no great issue of his ideas. He is an explorer feeling his way in an effort to reveal some unknown aspect of existence.'

That something might be revealed, and that this something might loosely be referred to as an idea, is perfectly possible – although Kundera himself despises that looseness and expresses his 'disgust for those who reduce a work to its ideas. My revulsion at being dragged into what they call "discussions of ideas". My despair at this era befogged with ideas and indifferent to works.' The difficulty and conflict arise when the novelist has designs on his readers' opinions *before* anything is revealed. The novel then risks becoming not an exploration or investigation, but an illustration of conclusions already reached, the fleshing out of abstractions. It is not hard to conceive how the desire to persuade might hedge your freedom in those moments when you sit with your feet up. The writing itself, the joyful surprise, the beauty, which Kundera celebrates as 'the suddenly kindled light of the never-before-said', is likely to come about, if at all, despite your convictions rather than because of them.

The problem with starting out with an idea you want to sell, however decent and ennobling it may be, is that it reverses the imaginative order from which the novel takes its life; a moral or political scheme draws you away at the very beginning, at the moment of inception, from the specific, from the detail, from the strange combination of details that give novels their curious power. When the specific becomes subservient to the scheme the expressive freedom that seems to be the very essence of this form is compromised.

This is not to say, to return again to the radiator and the tilted chair, that you can be without opinions, politics, the key to all mythologies, faith, nihilism, last night's dinner chat or what you will. You have the ragbag, just like everybody else. It will not go away, it is quietly helping you choose or discard your material. It will shape what you do because it is a part of what you are. But it is held in abeyance. It is not the foreground of consciousness. You enter a state of controlled passivity, you relax your grip and accept that even if your declared intention is to justify the ways of God to man, you might end up interesting your readers rather more in Satan.

Nor is this to say, and it is important to make this clear, that the novel should have nothing therefore to do with the vandalized, garbage-strewn arena of politics; on the contrary, it is precisely its expressive freedom and the capability it has of naming everything, exploring every corner of human experience, that make it a natural opponent of political systems, tyrannies and cant. The successful or memorable novels we think of as 'political' are always written *against* a politics. Satire, mockery, reduction to absurdity, direct attack or simply the detailed, remorseless naming of what is there, these are the novel's weapons against political, or for that matter, military or religious systems which restrict or deny human possibility. Consider this short list of novels which are likely to survive: Franz Kafka's *The Trial*, George Orwell's *1984*, Alexander Solzhenitsyn's *A Day in the Life of Ivan Denisovitch*, Joseph Heller's *Catch-22*, Milan Kundera's *The Book of Laughter and Forgetting*, Salman Rushdie's *The Satanic Verses*. All are written in defiance of a thought-system. None of them propounds a politics. None of these novelists offers up a total system to replace the one he attacks, or delivers a set of instructions by which we should live. Novelists know in their sceptical hearts that such instructions are precisely the danger, precisely the ineradicable human sickness. Instructions become instruments of domination, for there never seems to be a lack of people ready to enforce obedience to the Word or the Book, their word, their book.

Instead, what novelists can pit against the overbearing State, the organization or the bureaucracy are the values of the individual attempting, for example, to retain his or her identity, remaining or failing to remain loyal to friends, discovering the ascendancy of love or being crushed in the attempt. By measuring individual human worth, the novelist reveals the full enormity of the State's crime when it sets out to crush that individuality. The 'political' novel at its best, just like any other good novel, remains an open-ended voyage of exploration of experience; and not only the experience of the victim, but of his oppressor too. Tyranny has its roots and causes in human nature and this is the essential subject matter of the 'political' novelist.

It is for this reason that Milan Kundera has so fiercely resisted the label, 'political', as limiting and demeaning; and it was for related reasons I suspect, that George Orwell, in his *Inside the Whale*, celebrated Henry Miller's *Tropic of Cancer*. For those not familiar with Orwell's famous essay, it should be explained that 'inside the whale' refers to the situation of those writers who accept the world as it is and feel no wish to change it. They observe it but, 'in the dark cushioned space that exactly fits you, with yards of blubber between yourself and reality,' they do not engage with it.

As far as Orwell was concerned, political fiction did not carry the meaning I have been describing. He did not associate the political novel with anti-authoritarian subversion. Writing in 1940, looking back over a highly politicized decade, he had in mind writers of firm convictions on the right and left – 'cocksure partisans telling you what to think'. He was thinking particularly of his own generation which had embraced

Russian-led Communism, as a realizable Utopian ideal. 'Communists and near-Communists had a disproportionately large influence in the literary reviews. It was a time of labels, slogans and evasions. At the worst moments you were expected to lock yourself up in a constipating little cage of lies; at the best a sort of voluntary censorship ("Ought I say this? Is it pro-Fascist?").'

This atmosphere of orthodoxy 'is always damaging to prose, and above all it is completely ruinous to the novel, the most anarchical of all forms of literature'. For that reason he sees it as no coincidence that 'the best writers of the thirties have been poets'. For Orwell political writing was propagandist, bullying, cajoling, idea-dominated, lacking in human sympathies. Now, in 1940, those politics, and to Orwell, all politics, seemed to have failed. Europe was at war again, Nazi, Fascist and Stalinist tyrannies looked likely to obliterate its civilization. A new dark age was at hand.

Orwell, of course, was a man with a highly developed political awareness. What he saw in Miller's completely unpolitical novel, and, on a much grander scale in Joyce's *Ulysses*, was a vital preoccupation with the everyday, the common experience, the life of the 'ordinary man' and with 'sex and truthfulness about the inner life'. It was this truthfulness which he felt literature in its proselytizing infatuation with grand and morally bankrupt political schemes had betrayed. He wrote that 'Joyce dared – for it is a matter of daring just as much of technique – to expose the imbecilities of the inner mind, and in doing so he discovered an America which was under everybody's nose. Here is a whole world of stuff which you have lived with since childhood, stuff which you supposed to be of its nature incommunicable, and somebody has managed to communicate it.'

What Orwell missed in the literature and particularly the
novels of the thirties was a sceptical, open-minded approach.
In Miller's freewheeling cynicism he discovered a freedom
from cant and right-mindedness. In the same spirit he
lamented the fact that all the books in English about the
Spanish civil war were written from a political angle and
were dull. The same could not be said of the books that had
come out of the first world war – *All Quiet on the Western
Front, A Farewell to Arms, Goodbye to All That* – 'written
not by propagandists but by *victims*'. The novel as 'a product
of the free mind, of the autonomous individual' or at least the
good novel, could not be written in the atmosphere of the
thirties: 'Good novels are not written by orthodoxy-sniffers,
nor by people who are conscience-stricken about their own
unorthodoxy. Good novels are written by people who are *not
afraid*.'

This is the essential truth expressed in *Inside the Whale*, but
the essay is fascinating too in the ways in which Orwell
turned out to be wrong on other counts. *Tropic of Cancer*,
despite a number of quite brilliant passages, is not a major
novel, although, I believe, Miller's work is dismissed too
lightly these days. The decade which Orwell described as
being 'barren of imaginative prose' was a decade in which
Virginia Woolf for one, was writing novels. But then, since
she was not involved in politics in the sense in which Orwell
understood the word, she rather carries his point for him all
the same. European civilization survived in battered form.
The dark ages did not arrive, at least, not everywhere. The
'ordinary man' turned out to be not quite so passive as Orwell
feared. And most importantly, Orwell disregarded his own
recommendation to write 'inside the whale' like Miller, like
Joyce, and went on a few years later to swim way beyond
the confines of a blubbery belly and start work on his most

influential, though perhaps not his best book, *1984*. And yet what bridges this bleak, cautionary novel with the essay of 1940 is that all that Orwell had to pose against the mighty, stultifying, nightmare regime of Oceania is a man and a woman making love in a wood.

This man and woman, of course, are crushed in their attempt to defy the State. It is simply not the case, as Salman Rushdie contends in his spirited riposte to Orwell, *Outside the Whale*, that the pessimism of *1984*, by demonstrating the futility of resistance serves the interest of the status quo, of the masters If that were so, the Soviet Union among others, rather than ban it, would have made it compulsory reading long ago. No is it the case that Orwell's intellect and spirit were broken by the horrors of the age in which he lived. Terrifying state orthodoxies were crushing individuals in Orwell's time, and they have continued since, in Europe and elsewhere, in Iran today. It is not the first duty of the novelist to provide blueprints for insurrection, or uplifting tales of successful resistance for the benefit of the opposition. The naming of what is there is what is important. Orwell provided us with a vocabulary, an imaginative framework with which to describe and understand the numbing orthodoxy of a state tyranny, and how its first violence is against language itself. If Winston Smith had brought down the State, *1984* would have lost its savage and cautionary power. It would have become a fantasy, an adventure story; a man in love does not bring down a social system. And if, in the interests of plausibility, it was Winston along with a heroic and tightly organized political organization which rose up triumphantly against Big Brother, the novel would have lost its vital involvement with an individual fate, and become an enfeebled manipulation of political reality.

Orwell had the courage of his pessimism. He was not going

to join the 'cocksure partisans'. What he also brought to *1984* from *Inside the Whale* was an insistence on detailed description of the ordinary, the everyday. It is the cabbage smells, the grit-laden wind, the blunt razor blades, the disgusting, crumbly tobacco, the corruscating Victory Gin which one remembers better than the workings, say, of the Ministries. The novel tends to buckle under the weight of the task of evoking a whole functioning social system; when descriptions of institutions have to double as tacit condemnations, then authorial intention tends to stand in the way of inspiration. For it is of course, still, a very moral book, its pessimism cannot, nor is it intended to, deliver it from that. Pessimism is just one of morality's techniques.

The novels we think of as political seem, then, to offer only frail testimony against the self-generating 'truths' of politicians; the ideas, the messages, the concealed exhortations when they have been ripped from the body of the text for purposes of easier discussion are little more than bloodied banalities: totalitarianism is inhuman and absurd, war is barbaric, bureaucracies crush individuals. You can see novelists, all novelists, not just the politically inclined, wince when they are asked, But what is your novel really *about*? They either turn away from the question, which generally means from all questions, or become practised at a certain kind of wind storm of words, a self-protecting blather. Try repeating it thrice daily at publication time, and the feeling of betraying the work itself is as palpable as a bad dose of 'flu.

But that frailty is deceptive. Take the example of *The Satanic Verses*. The average Briton rarely sees the inside of a church, and is so far removed from matters of that sort that he hardly bothers to call himself an atheist. To need to do that you would have to have some believers around. Suppose he was

shown that book of revelations, specific directions and strict
admonitions known as the Koran, and then he was offered
the opinion that the source of these words was not God
speaking through Mohammed, but Mohammed, thinking it all
up for himself and his followers. Our man would be unlikely
to take exception; he might even think it was a perfectly
sensible explanation. And if he wrote the opinion down
himself on a piece of paper and photocopied it and passed it
around in the High Street, I doubt if there is a Moslem in
the land who would bother to reach for his matches. Moslems
would know the statement to be untrue, and beyond
contempt.

But what happens when that opinion becomes transmogrified
and stitched in to a larger tapestry, and the dissenting fabulist
is an ex-Moslem himself, perhaps bitter, or more likely,
gleeful in the demonstration of limitless freedoms? Once a
Moslem, there were things not to be said. But not now. Now
it is the re-telling of the old story, now it is slang, street
wisdom, tough-guy metaphysics, comic book leaps, Koranic
parody, solemn narration. The angel Gibreel dreams of
Gibreel on the mountain top, and Mohammed-Mahound,
toiling up towards him will have to be played by Gibreel
too, and the force that works Gibreel's jaw comes from
Mahound, along the shining cord of light that connects them,
navel to navel, while Gibreel, scared silly, hangs in the sky
like a kite – 'Mahound's eyes open wide, he's seeing some
kind of vision, staring at it, oh, that's right, Gibreel
remembers, me. He's seeing me. My lips moving, being
moved by. What, whom? Don't know, can't say. Nevertheless,
here they are, coming out of my mouth, up my throat, past
my teeth: the Words.'

The idea, is only an unremarkable heresy. The true testimony
against the strictures of Islam in *The Satanic Verses* is in

Rushdie's method, and most importantly, in his choice of literary form. A dissenting tract would never have caused such a fuss; such works, often scholarly books, are simply and efficiently banned in Moslem countries. Here the dissent is in the telling, in the celebration of imaginative possibility, in the freedom to assume and discard voices, points of view, tones of voice; it is the riotous assembly of imagined and historical personages. It was not the intellectual traditions of Islam which granted these freedoms.

And it is these qualities, rather than reducible ideas or encoded messages, that a novel at its best has at its command when it finds itself the adversary of a thought system. The very form of the novel, or the very nature of the possibilities it affords – imaginatively pluralistic, humanistic, intrigued by the fate of individuals, sceptical – suggests a clamorous democracy; anyone might become central to the story, every point of view must be heard. The freely conceived novel sits as uneasily with the Czechoslovakian state apparatus as it does with Islamic fundamentalism. If you want to argue with Caesar on Caesar's terms, then you had better write expository prose in which to propound in the clearest terms your vision of an alternative social order. But if you want to understand Caesar, and why he recurs and how we are in him as much as he is in us, then tilt back your chair . . .

During 1980 and 1981 I was attempting to begin a new novel. I had no end of energy, inclination and time, and I had a number of pieces I knew belonged together. But I was discovering that my thoughts were not free. A new cold war had begun, and it frightened and angered me. I was being distracted to such an extent that I set aside my few pages and decided to make this my subject. At first sight it looked promising – public policy, private fear – the kind of opposition I like. The Soviet Union was deploying a new missile along its western borders, it had invaded Afghanistan, and looked like it might move in on Poland. A new American President was calling for an armament programme of unbelievable proportions. A war or words had begun, the atmosphere was edgy, nervous, the two contestants were full of swagger. Across Europe, and a little later in the United States there were public demonstrations of opposition to the new arms race, gatherings of quite unprecedented size, a quarter, a half a million in many capitals. The anxiety was widespread and deep. Many people I spoke to complained of dreams, nightmares of nuclear war.

I had facts and figures. I knew about warhead counts, and MIRVing, and MAD and SALT and hardened silos, smart weapons, improved accuracy, and the precarious differences between strategic, tactical and battlefield nuclear weapons. I discovered the eerily calm academic field of nuclear strategy and deterrence theory and I read back through its changing fashions, and through the moves and counter moves of the arms race itself. I found out about the likely effect of a one megaton airburst as against a groundburst on a large city, and about the prospects for life on earth after an all-out nuclear exchange. Then there was Hiroshima and Nagasaki to re-discover, this time in detail, and Oppenheimer and General Groves and the Manhattan project. Then the thing itself going off, the awesome cliché of the mushroom cloud, the flash, the magnetic pulse, the radiation burn, the radiation sickness, the fall-out, the contamination, the half-life counted in thousands of years. The Bomb was a subject in itself, you could almost forget it while studying it. I could have taken a degree in it. Perhaps in some mid-Western college it might have been possible.

In addition to the burden of facts, was the burden of morality. To loathe these weapons was hardly the point. Even the

most ferocious proponents of the new arms race were happy
to admit their horror of nuclear war; that was why we needed
more and better weapons, to deter the other side from the
'unthinkable'. Moral revulsion, openly or tacitly expressed
was not sufficient. I wanted to go a little further and discover
what possible grounds there could be for hope that we might
in the long term not simply muddle through, but surmount
the problem we had set ourselves. The conventional politics
of arms agreements, the Test Ban Treaty and the SALT
agreements had offered ways of managing the arms race
rather than preventing it. I was thinking beyond politics to
the slender possibility, and it did seem the only long term
hope, that a transformation would have to occur, not in
governments but in individuals, in our understanding of our
place in the natural world; if we were to avoid destroying the
world we would have to become participators and sharers in
creation, rather than masters and exploiters of it. The
construct of this change, represented by a shift from a
Newtonian to an Einsteinian world view, or, in more general
terms, from a masculine to a feminine consciousness or
emphasis in our civilization, is a matter I discussed in the
introduction reprinted here. It draws, of course, on writings
of the women's movement, and on discussions of the new
physics which in turn were so influenced.

Armed to the teeth with my facts and figures, histories, moral
revulsion and precarious moral hopes, desperate to engage
and persuade everybody in what I took to be the single most
important issue to face humankind, I was all set to write the
worst novel imaginable. I could barely move for facts and
opinions. It seemed as though I had thought of everything
and felt too much. I could not imagine surprising myself. Too
much thought had left me with too little imaginative
freedom. I could make no pleasurable discoveries in writing.

My baggage was too heavy, and I was stuck. When Michael Berkeley asked me if I would like to write him the words for an oratorio, I agreed immediately. I left the luggage standing there, picked up my overnight bag and ran.

Choosing a new form in which to write bears some resemblance to travelling abroad; the sense of freedom is no less useful for being illusory or temporary. The new place has its own rules and conventions, but they are not really yours, not quite yet. What you notice first is the absence of the old, familiar constraints, and you do things you would not do at home. I wrote in the introduction of the freedoms I found in the limited form of the libretto; essentially, I had a moral argument to make of which I was not ashamed, and in words that were to be set to music, I could carry that argument directly and without embarrassment.

In ten years the atmosphere has changed greatly, thanks largely to the rise of Mr Gorbachev and the accompanying revolution in Soviet foreign policy, and partly to the pressure of public opinion in the West which has made even President Reagan, the only begetter of the not quite forgotten Strategic Defense Initiative, grasp that it is a matter of no great dishonour to be seen signing an arms reduction agreement. The atmosphere has lightened, but the underlying situation remains unchanged. The INF treaty had more political than military significance; it was the first agreement between the two sides actually to reduce their arsenals, but it affected only three or four per cent of the world stockpile. The silos, the missiles, the nuclear submarines, the complex, computer-controlled command centres are all still there, still ready, at a moment's notice to eradicate life on earth in less than an hour. A year after the signing of the INF treaty, the Americans put their radar-undetectable Stealth bomber on public display. Both the United States and the Soviet Union have continued their research and development programmes for the militarization of space, and the oceans of the world are now thoroughly militarized in this respect. Great Britain is about to undergo a thirty-fold increase in its nuclear firepower, and the campaign is warming up to persuade the NATO members to modernize their nuclear weapons.

The civil nuclear programme, the source of essential weapons-quality plutonium, has been expanding in this country and is beginning to revive in the United States. Nuclear proliferation is now a familiar litany – Argentina, Brazil, Pakistan, Israel, India, South Africa . . . The deep unreason of all this continuing activity, an unreason which I must assume is common to us all, was illustrated afresh by the Chernobyl catastrophe, a point made at the time by I. F. Stone, writing in the *The Nation*. The radioactive fallout from that accident was equivalent to that of a smallish H-bomb. The scale of the environmental damage *outside* the Soviet Union as prevailing winds carried radioactivity across Western Europe to northern Scotland demonstrates the futility of our launching such a weapon against an enemy; we might not be the first to suffer, but we certainly would be the second.

The obsessive deployment of more effective nuclear weapons is just one aspect of our brutal and arrogant threat to the natural world of which, of course, we are only a part, and whose processes sustain us. During this decade there was established an even more familiar litany, and to type out even a fraction of it is wearisome: the destruction of rain forests, of plant and animal species, of the ozone layer, the now inevitable and possibly catastrophic rise in the earth's temperature, the pollution of rivers, lakes and oceans by chemical and radioactive waste, the aesthetic and environmental nightmare of industrialized agriculture . . . Our assault on nature has been vigorous and thorough; as the soprano sings in the final section, 'Grieving moon, do our virile times suggest to you the metaphor of rape . . .?' Governments sponsor conferences or issue ringing statements, or tamper with the presentation of their policies to accommodate the anxieties of their electorates, but so far no government has even contemplated the redirection of its economy in the face of these problems, no major political party of the left or right has begun to think of breaking with the doomed fixation on endless economic growth. The question remains open – shall we change, shall there be womanly times, or shall we die?

In the first half of this century, in the industrial democracies of Western Europe and in the United States, a majority of working people voted for and benefitted enormously from socialist or liberal policies which, in the face of powerful opposition, aimed at a degree of wealth distribution and at the organization of free health care and education, and unemployment and social security provision. Over the years some of the very cruellest effects of poverty were dulled, and social provision came to be accepted by all parties as one of the responsibilities of government. As the majority of the working population became relatively prosperous, voters began to favour the political party whose first priority was the retention or increase of that prosperity. The party whose natural constituency was the large minority still struggling with the basics, tended to find itself in opposition. This shift has been noticeable in many countries over the past fifteen years. In Britain the change was rather spectacular. The new spirit of private prosperity was personified right from the beginning of the eighties by an energetic populist leader whose government coincided with a divided opposition and large oil revenues with which to subsidize mass unemployment and a consumer boom.

In a very short time, Great Britain began to feel like a quite different place as this new spirit took hold. Money-obsessed, aggressively competitive and individualistic, contemptuous of the weak, vindictive towards the poor, favouring the old American opposition of private affluence and public squalor, and individual gain against communal solutions, indifferent to the environment, deeply philistine, enamoured of policemen, soldiers and weapons – virile times indeed. And interesting times too. I was fascinated by the changes. I could not believe that this transformation could be entirely the work of Mrs Thatcher and her government. Something had been released in people, something that was both acquisitive and fearful. A fear perhaps of being left behind in the scramble. I wanted to catch something of all this and leave it free to condemn itself. At the same time I had some rather too well-formed thoughts on history and memory, and public and private morality – again there seemed good reasons for finding a form other than the novel.

I am not really certain why writing dialogue in play form should encourage an engagement with social conflicts and values. I had certainly found this to be the case when I wrote a television film for Richard Eyre, *The Imitation Game*, which was a polemic about gender and power. Perhaps when the page you are working on contains nothing more than what people say and do you are drawn into behaviour and motive, and through them to underlying values. It could be that writing dialogue in this way, instructions to actors, is more mimetic, a more narrowly accurate representation of the surface of social existence than that afforded by the novel with all its conventional freedoms of, for example, authorial intrusion, and the highly artificial depiction of the inner life.

It could be simply a matter of recent usage; in the seventies particularly, many of my contemporaries who were playwrights wrote about their times with a directness that was not available to fiction writers, certainly not to me. Fiction is more personal than play or screenplay writing; the novel is not best suited to topical issues, or catching on the wing a changing social mood. Novels take longer to cook.

The Ploughman's Lunch incorporated some events even as they unfolded. It started out as a story about a man who denies his own past and attempts to lie his way into a love affair while setting about the opportunistic rewriting of the history of the Suez crisis. It ended up concerning itself also with immediate questions of national identity; shortly after I finished the first draft, Parliament had its famous Saturday morning debate, and the Fleet was dispatched to the Falkland Islands. In retrospect the film seems very much part of that early moment of triumphant consolidation – Mrs Thatcher's popularity was low before the war, and has remained more or less high ever since.

In the summer of 1983, two months after *The Ploughman's Lunch* had been released, I found myself tilting my chair and daydreaming about a novel I might write. I began to make notes. I was about to become a father, and my thoughts were narrowed and intensified. I was haunted by the memory, or perhaps the memory of a dream, of a footpath that emerges onto a bend in a country road. It is luxuriant high summer, and there is a fine drizzle. There is a pub just along the road. A figure who is me and not me is walking towards it, certain that he is about to witness something of overwhelming importance. Writing *The Child in Time*, which took me to the end of 1986, was about the discovery of what that man saw. Other elements – a man pulled from the wreckage of a lorry, a birth, a lost child, a man who attempts to return to his childhood, an authoritarian childcare handbook, the elusive and protean nature of time – all these seemed to rotate about this central scene, and would somehow explain it, or contribute to it. In other words, I had a detail, a country road on a certain day, an echo whose apparent urgency was its only justification, and this seemed the proper starting point for a novel; where the oratorio and the film began with an intention to engage and persuade, here I had a fragment whose appeal I was not yet able to explain.

At the same time, I could not have written *The Child in Time* without having written the preceding two pieces. I had never been the kind of novelist who was drawn to describing or implying a society. *The Ploughman's Lunch* gave me some basis for an attempt. In my research for the oratorio and its introduction I had come across accounts of contemporary physics and its diverse and extraordinary explanations of the nature of time, and from the oratorio itself I carried over a belief in the insufficiency of the intellect alone in understanding ourselves or our world. When the *The Child in Time* was published in 1987 I was surprised to read in many places that I was breaking a six year silence since my novel, *The Comfort of Strangers*. The readers of novels, music audiences and movie goers do not overlap as much as I had thought. From my point of view there was no silence, only a tactical evasion, a move abroad; the novel is a capacious form, but not everything is appropriate to it.

1989

or Shall We Die?

Words of an oratorio set to music
by Michael Berkeley

For
Polly and Alice
and all children

Introduction

The subject matter of this oratorio seemed more of an inevitability than a choice. Throughout 1980, along with many others, I found myself disturbed and obsessed by the prospect of a new and madly vigorous arms race. Russia had recently invaded Afghanistan and later in the year there was the possibility of intervention later in Poland. In the United States public opinion, or media opinion – the two are sometimes hard to separate – was demanding a restoration of American might after the perceived humiliation of the Iranian hostage crisis, and by the end of the year a new president had been elected who promised a programme of weapon manufacture on a scale without precedent. In this country the government was committed to increasing and 'improving' our nuclear capability. The Russians meanwhile were steadily deploying their SS 20 missiles. The language of the nuclear apologists had taken a fresh turn: there was open talk of a limited and winnable nuclear war in which Europe would serve as a battleground for the two major powers. Weapons had been devised accordingly. The fragile concept of deterrence had been shaken by the determination on both sides to find ever more accurate missiles that could hit enemy silos – weapons that were only of use in a first strike, before the enemy could empty its silos.

One turned in vain to the history books to discover a time when nations prepared so extensively for war and none had happened. And yet between East and West there were no obvious territorial disputes. Despite scare stories to the contrary, there was no ruthless competition for diminishing resources. And the extent of the mutual dependence for new markets and new technology was so great as to undermine any pretence of a genuine ideological conflict. It was as if each side prepared for war because it saw the other doing the same. The governments of each side had much in common, as did their civilian populations who were united by the prospect of annihilation and – in attitude – by their indifference, or by their helplessness and fear. For all the complex discussion of nuclear strategy with its unique blend of logic and paranoia, at heart the situation had about it the aspect of very simple human folly. To call it childish would be to demean children, who would soon tire of such a game: I'm getting ready to hit you because you are getting ready to hit me. That this madness, which threatens not only human life, present and future, but all life on the planet, should be presented on our television screens as sanity, as responsible deliberation on 'defence' policy by calm, authoritative men in suits, gave the matter the quality of a nightmare; either they were completely mad, or we were. Ultimately, however, I believe their madness is ours, and the responsibility for survival is a collective one.

The widespread apprehension experienced in 1980 brought about large-scale public opposition in Europe and later in the United States. Now three-quarters of all Americans appear to favour some form of freeze on weapon construction, and peace movements can claim to have modified, at least, the rhetoric of politicians. For all that, the arms race continues. New weapon systems are to be introduced across Europe during 1983, and the Russians have continued to deploy their medium-range missiles. Public opposition has had only minimal effect on policy, but its importance is greater than its effect – that opposition represents all the hope there is.

Public opposition, of course, had its roots in private fears, and in 1980 I was struck by how deeply the lives of individuals had been shaken by the new cold war. It was precisely this that made me want to write about it. Those who were parents, or had children in their lives, seemed particularly affected. Love of children generates a fierce ambition for the world to continue and be safe, and makes one painfully vulnerable to fantasies of loss. Like others, I experienced the jolt of panic that wakes you before dawn, the daydreams of the mad rush of people and cars out of the city before it is destroyed, of losing a child in the confusion. People described the pointlessness of planning ahead, a creeping sense of the irrelevance of all the things they valued against the threat of annihilation. Helplessness generated anger, which in turn threatened friendships. Images of nuclear war invaded dreams. As in war itself, matters of public policy had profound consequences for private lives.

For most people the panic could not last. A kind of numbness descends, and we have a saving – or is it fatal? – ability to compartmentalize, to keep dread in one room, hope or indifference in another. The threat remains, we continue to deplore it, a few of us take action, but life goes on, thankfully, and most of us learn to sleep again without nightmares.

I wanted to write about those private fears while they were still fresh. I thought the subject matter was best suited to film. I wrote outlines and abandoned them. I sketched out the opening chapters of a novel – but in all these attempts I felt defeated by scale; the problem was at once so colossal and so human. How could it be made to fit? And yet as soon as Michael Berkeley asked me to consider writing a libretto

for an oratorio, I felt certain that this could be a way of
approaching the subject. Music would at once translate it to
another realm, abstract, beyond definitions, and yet with
direct appeal to feelings. Michael Berkeley's music, and
especially his oboe concerto, had affected me enormously:
though its textures and complexities were undeniably
contemporary, his was also an accessible music, often
rhythmically exciting, with expressive melodies. His music
had the power to move. He belonged to a tradition of English
composers who have drawn inspiration from their country's
literature. He had written settings of poems by Donne,
Herbert, Lewis Carroll and Hardy, among others, and had
composed a particularly beautiful piece for piano inspired by
Wilfred Owen's poem 'Strange Meeting'. Above all, it turned
out that he shared my feelings about the urgency of the subject
matter. He introduced me to Tippett's oratorio *A Child of
Our Time*, written in the thirties when another war in Europe
was a growing possibility. The Mother in this work certainly
influenced the presence of the mother in my libretto.

One immediate attraction of an oratorio was purely formal;
a man's voice set against a woman's, and both set against a
choir, addressing a matter of moral and spiritual crisis by
singing about it directly, without the complications of a
dramatic setting, and in terms that could be alternately public
or intimate – there was a purity about this that was appealing.
No characters, no psychology, no actors pretending to be
other people, simply voices articulating profoundest fears
and some hope. There was too the challenge, as I saw it, of
writing a singable English, simple and clear, that could
express public themes without pomposity and private feelings
without bathos. As it turned out, *or Shall We Die?* took on
a certain amount of dramatic shape since the voices assume a
number of different roles, though these are not sufficiently

defined to be characters. And whether the oratorio's language is clear or singable will not be discovered until the first performance, which is still some months ahead as I write.

Traditionally, an oratorio is a non-dramatic choral work that addresses a religious theme. Clearly it could be extended to include moral, political or even private themes, and there is, in fact, a well-established secular tradition. The oratorio, rather like the novel, is more a term of convenience than of precise definition. To present at the beginning of this secular oratorio the idea of a mother and child may seem a deliberate and even too obvious an invocation of the form's religious tradition. Tippett was an influence, but often it is only in retrospect that one realizes how one's choices may be influenced by a particular work one admires, and powerfully shaped by archetypal forms. At the time of writing I thought of the woman who sings the first section as an exact contemporary of mine, someone I might know well – a woman not necessarily given to millennial thoughts, who delights in a clear summer's evening and remembers, precisely at the moment of her greatest joy, the threat of war.

She may have heard of or read accounts of the bombing of Hiroshima. Mrs Tomoyasu was a young woman in 1945 whose nine-year-old daughter died in her arms. She told her story to Jonathan Dimbleby in his film *In Evidence: the Bomb* and I am indebted to him, and to Mrs Tomoyasu and to Yorkshire Television, for the use of her words – changed only to make smoother rhythms – in section five. Although Mrs Tomoyasu's terrible experience is almost forty years in the past, I thought of it as a ghostly prefiguration in section one, the starkest embodiment of what we most fear from nuclear strategy.

During the time I spent considering exactly how the oratorio should proceed, I speculated that if there was intelligent life elsewhere in the universe, it was likely that sooner or later it

would discover that matter and energy are not distinct entities
but lie along a continuum. For civilizations without high
technology the discovery would pose no threat. Long before
Einstein's theories, the Chinese term for physics was *Wu Li*,
in which the Word *Wu* can mean either matter or energy. The
identification of the two has long been a feature of eastern
religions. In the Mundaka Upanishad it says: 'By energism of
consciousness, Brahman is massed; from that Matter is born
and from Matter, Life, Mind and the Worlds.' For those
civilizations with technology, on the other hand, the means
for total self-destruction would become available. It is as if
nuclear energy is a kind of evolutionary filter, and this is the
argument of the second section. Of those civilizations who
make the discovery, only those who do not build the weapons
or, less likely, build them and do not use them, survive to
evolve further.

Later I discovered that this speculation of mine was at least
as old as nuclear weapons. I heard one scientist fantasize
about speeding time up to such an extent that one could look
out across the universe and see countless pinprick flares of
intelligent civilizations destroying themselves because their
cleverness had outrun their wisdom.

From this remote perspective, the existence of nuclear
weapons not only threatens but also indicts us all. It is not
simply a matter of what governments do to us, but of what
we are, and what we could become. If there is to be no
nuclear war it will be because a sufficient number of people,
inside and outside governments, set about securing this end. In
the final resort the responsibility is for the species as a whole.
If our evolutionary test defeats us, it will defeat us all.

The first nuclear weapons were developed in the early 1940s
and built for use against the Germans. By the time the first
bombs were ready, Germany had surrendered and instead the

inhabitants of Hiroshima and Nagasaki became the first
victims of nuclear attack. It was by no means an inevitable
choice. Reading the minutes of the committees set up to
advise the American President on the use of the bomb, and
reading the accounts of the deliberations of various interested
groups, I was surprised by the extent of the opposition to
the use of the bomb against civilians, and by the humanity
and farsightedness of the arguments deployed. There were
numerous proposals; dropping the bomb in the desert or the
ocean with Japanese observers present was one line of
approach, discounted for many reasons. The US Navy was
convinced that a blockade would bring a Japanese surrender
within months. Japan's industrial output was a fraction of its
pre-war figure, and raw materials were virtually non-existent.
There was one forcefully argued case for dropping the bomb
on a huge forest of cryptomeria trees not far from Tokyo.
The trees would be felled along the line of blast, and the
power of a single bomb would be evident. Beyond all this,
intercepted and deciphered radio traffic suggested that
powerful figures in the Japanese military, with access to the
Emperor, were convinced that Japan could not win the war
and were seeking a surrender – albeit a conditional surrender
that would salvage some degree of national dignity. There
were those in the US administration who argued that in this
instance the difference between conditional and unconditional
surrender was little more than verbal, and that with some
flexibility the war could be ended by diplomatic means.

However, the bomb seemed to have had its own momentum.
It was a triumph of theoretical and technological daring. The
scientists working on the project were so involved in solving
countless problems, and so elated when they succeeded, that
many of them lost touch with the ultimate goal of their labours
– colossal destruction. The bomb was a pinnacle of human

achievement – intellect divorced from feeling – and there appears to have been a deep, collective desire to see it used, despite all arguments. Opponents of its use were always on the defensive. Furthermore, at the beginning of the war, genocide had been the strategy of the Axis powers alone. By 1945 it had become acceptable to all combatants; fascism had to be defeated by fascism's methods, and the mass destruction at Hiroshima and Nagasaki had powerful precedents in the fire bombing of Dresden and Tokyo.

The nuclear bombing of these two cities, then, was not purely the responsibility of a handful of genocidally inclined military advisers; it was made possible by a general state of mind, by a deep fascination with technological solutions, by judgments barbarized by warfare and by nations which – rightly or wrongly – had organized themselves to inflict destruction. The public, when it heard the news of the bombing, though shocked was by no means overwhelmingly critical. Ever since that time, attempts to prevent the proliferation of nuclear weapons have been a total failure. There are now more than sixty thousand nuclear warheads, primed and programmed for their destinations. The smaller of these are vastly more powerful than the Hiroshima bomb. If, as a species, we faced a simple test of wisdom, from the very outset we appeared to be intent on failure.

Before the slaughter there never seems to be a priest lacking to bless the executioners. The chorus's lines in section three reflect my conviction that whatever moral or spiritual resources are necessary for us to avoid destroying ourselves they are unlikely to be provided by the world-weary bureaucracies of the established churches, nor by any religious sect that claims that it alone has the ear of God. If, for example, the Church of England comes to accept, as is likely, the idea that within women as well as men there is a spiritual dimension that could enable them to become priests, it will be less from conviction than from tired capitulation to changes in the secular world. In the same way, the Church may follow the opposition to militarism but never – as an institution – lead it. This is not to deny, of course, that many exceptional individuals work within that and other churches. But centuries of mind-numbing dogma, professionalization and enmeshment in privilege have all but annihilated the mystical and spiritual experience that is said to be at the heart of Christianity.

During the first thirty years of this century there occurred a scientific revolution whose significance we are only now beginning to understand, for its repercussions are not confined to science. Space, time, matter, energy, light, all came to be thought of in entirely new ways, and ultimately must affect the way we see the world and our place within it. We continue, of course, to live within a Newtonian universe – its physics are perfectly adequate to describe and measure the world we can see; only the very large and the very small are beyond its grasp. More importantly, our habits of mind, our intellectual and moral frameworks, are consonant with the Newtonian world-view. The impartial observer of Newtonian thought is so pervasive a presence in all our thinking that it is difficult to describe this 'commonsense' world in anything but its terms. Detachment is a characteristic we value highly in intellectual activity, so too is objectivity. In our medicine we describe the human personality as a static structure (super-ego, ego, id) and the body as a vastly complicated clock whose individual parts can be treated in isolation when they fail. We conceive of ourselves moving through time in an orderly, linear fashion in which cause invariably precedes effect. When it appears not to, as in, say, a precognitive dream, we are quick to dismiss the experience, or ridicule as superstitious those who do not. We frequently describe the world as though we ourselves were invisible. Environments are planned – from tower blocks to new social orders – as though people *en masse* are utterly distinct from the planners, and can be acted upon and shaped like clay. Though we recognize the line of our descent, for the most part we consider other animals as little more than automata to be experimented on or destroyed as we require. We stand separate from our world – and from ourselves and from each other – describing, measuring, shaping it like gods.

The insufficiency of this paradigm – knowledge as 'mastery' of the unknown – is expressed in the final section and in section four a kind of battle hymn celebrates ironically the most aggressive form of this world-view. Logic, discipline, objectivity, thought unmuddied by emotion, are qualities traditionally associated with the male, and patriarchal values are celebrated here in the same manner. Because governments have never sought public opinion on nuclear policy until after that policy has been shaped, and because of the cult of secrecy that surrounds them, nuclear weapons are represented here as powerfully subversive of democratic procedures.

Only when I had finished a first draft of the libretto did it occur to me to insert the stanzas from William Blake's 'The Tyger', 'A Divine Image', and 'The Divine Image'. This particularly pleased Michael Berkeley whose piece for Soprano and Orchestra, *The Wild Winds*, was a setting of Blake's 'Mad Song'. We came to think of these additions as chorales. Blake was a powerful opponent of Newtonian science, and his poetry returns again and again to the perils of divorcing reason from feeling; inseparable from these polarities were the male and female principles which take many forms in his writing. Since I could never aspire to Blake's density of meaning or the simplicity and beauty of his expression, I decided to draw on his strength by quotation and to think of him as the presiding spirit of the piece.

One can only speculate about a world-view that would be entirely consonant with the discoveries of the scientific revolution of this century. It hardly seems possible that what is now orthodox in science should continue for ever to be so much at odds with what we now hold to be commonsense. Objectivity does not exist in quantum mechanics. The observer is a part of what he observes. Reality is changed by the presence of the observer – he can no longer pretend to be invisible. Matter can no longer be thought of as being composed of minute, hard 'bits'; sub-atomic particles are now seen in terms of their tendency to exist, or as fields of energy. The stuff of matter has become the stuff of mind. As one commentator* has written, 'We are a part of nature, and when we study nature there is no way round the fact that nature is studying itself . . .' Physics could be regarded as 'the study of the structure of consciousness'. Niels Bohr's Theory of Complementarity – as far as I can grasp it – explains that we do not study the world so much as study our interaction with it. Without us the object of study (light, for example) does not exist. Conversely, without a world to interact with, we do not exist.

Increasingly the talk of physicists has come to sound like theology. Their theories and experiments have caused them t place consciousness at the centre of their concerns, and in many sacred texts they find their new understanding eloquently mirrored or extended. Some physicists are speculating about the ultimate identity of thought and matter. The new physics finds itself in the realm of the

* G. Zukav, *The Dancing Wu Li Masters*, Hutchinson, London, 1979

ineffable. The supreme intellectual achievement of western civilization, and its most potent shaping force – science – has perhaps reached a point where it might no longer be at odds with that deep intuitive sense – which seems to have been always with us – that there is a spiritual dimension to our existence, that there is a level of consciousness within us at which a transcendent unity may be perceived and experienced. It would be arrogant of scientists to believe that they might now be able to give some credence to religious experience, or that it is for them to ratify or disprove in their laboratories the teachings of yogis. No one who takes his or her own thoughts seriously has not asked, in some form or other, Tolstoy's great question: 'Is there any meaning in my life that the inevitable death awaiting me does not destroy?' Previously scientists have claimed that the question lies outside their brief, or have been quick to answer in the negative. Now some physicists are claiming an openness and humility towards religious texts that their predecessors would have found extraordinary.

I believe there are signs that the new physics has begun to be paralleled in many of the ways we study ourselves and our world – the two are no longer so distinct. Whether these emergent signs will ever become dominant, whether they could coalesce into a world-view that could transform our perception of everyday reality, is an open question. To bind intellect to our deepest intuition, to dissolve the sterile division between what is 'out there' and what is 'in here', to grasp that the *Tao*, our science and our art describe the same reality – to be whole – would be to be incapable of devising or dropping a nuclear bomb. How paradoxical that a scientific revolution should now suggest ways in which we might outgrow our materialism and dualism. In the great resurgence of interest in mysticism, eastern philosophies, ancient forms of divination and healing, it would be wrong to see only a fashionable escapism from the orthodoxies of rational scepticism; whether sublimely or inarticulately expressed, this interest represents a sure sense of the limitations of these orthodoxies, and a certainty that not all private experience is explained satisfactorily in materialist terms. Belief in the untapped resources of consciousness is radically reshaping our psychologies and therapies. Holism is a powerful influence too in many fields; holistic medicine and many forms of healing that lie outside the mechanistic approach of conventional medicine stress the consciousness of the practitioner as well as that of the patient, and regard them as interpenetrating. The growing science of ecology places us firmly within the intricate systems of the natural world and warns us that we may yet destroy what sustains us.

One could characterize these two world-views – the Newtonian and that of the new physics – as representing a male and female principle, yang and yin. In the Newtonian universe, there is objectivity; its impartial observer is logical and imagines himself to be all-seeing and invisible; he believes that if he had access to all facts, then everything could be explained. The observer in the Einsteinian universe believes herself to be part of the nature she studies, part of its constant flux; her own consciousness and the surrounding world pervade each other and are interdependent; she knows that at the heart of things there are limitations and paradoxes (the speed of light, the Uncertainty Principle) that prevent her from knowing or expressing everything; she has no illusions of her omniscience, and yet her power is limitless because it does not reside in her alone.

'Shall there be womanly times, or shall we die?' I believe the options to be as stark as that. Could we dare hope that we stand on the threshold of rethinking our world-view so radically that we might confront an evolutionary transformation of consciousness? It may seem a remote possibility, but then it is no more absurd a hope than that we will somehow muddle through. Perhaps less so, for violence is so dominant a feature of our civilization that failing change it seems unavoidable that sooner or later these weapons – all the power of the new physics at the command of Newtonian ambition – will be fired. Nor is there anything in our recent history to make me believe that in great, compassionate schemes of planning and reorganization we could engineer social systems that would somehow make nuclear war unthinkable or unnecessary.

Ultimately the change must come within individuals in sufficient numbers. The dominant theme would have to shift from violence to nurture. Children, not oil or coal or nuclear energy, are our most important resource, and yet we could hardly claim that our culture is organized round their needs. Our education system alone, with its absurd elitism is sufficient demonstration of our betrayal of their potential.

Could we ever learn to 'live lightly on the earth', using the full range of our technological resources, but using them in harmony and balance with our environment rather than in crude violation of it? To desire a given outcome is not sufficient reason for believing it will transpire. If we are free to change, then we are also free to fail. My own belief in the future fluctuates. There are sudden insights into the love and inventiveness of individuals to give me hope for all humankind; and then there are acts of cruelty and destruction that make me despair.

I. M.
London, September 1982

One

WOMAN
Midsummer . . . midnight.
I left my daughter sleeping and climbed
the hill behind our house to watch the sky.

The bright swarm of the Milky Way.
What stars! What simple joy to see and name them.
I found Orion, Pleiades, the Kids.

A nightjar sang. In the house below
my daughter slept. By her window was a tree.
A fresh wind stirred its leaves. My joy
engulfed the house, the land on which it lay,
the dome of infinite stars.

And even now, as I sit upon the grass,
across the world, in buried places,
sleepless men wait at consoles and watch
the patient sweep of scanners for a sign of penetration,
male virgins, deathmasks in the greenish light.

They and their masters have taken into custody
our lives, all life, my daughter, the nightjar,
the grass beneath my hands.

They and their enemies are men alike;
our enemy is their innocence.

How shall I reconcile this summer's night
with the troubled dreams of all my friends,
with a daughter in a book, dying
in her mother's arms, the dread in every voice?

My daughter, deep love breeds fear of loss.
I look back towards the house.

My heart, and the night's heart, are racing,
as though our world has held its breath
too long, too long.

Two

CHORUS
On distant stars the laws of mathematics hold.

The velocity of light is constant.

MAN
On countless lonely planets intelligent life
evolves, observes and measures the universe,
questions its beginnings, and discovers at last
by theory and by observation the power
locked in matter that causes suns to burn
for near eternity.

CHORUS
Matter and energy, body and spirit,
the benevolent unity, so simple to intuit,
so difficult to sift.

MAN
On countless planets that power locked in
matter is traced to larger patterns,
the measurements resume in wonder.

But lesser forms, intent on conquest,
helplessly construct the means of their destruction,
and then must face a simple test of wisdom.

CHORUS
Shall we pass, or shall we die?

Three

MAN

Our load was heavy, the aircraft slow to lift.
The night turned grey, then palest pink.
The unblemished ocean softened in the morning haze.

CHORUS

The aircrew kneels before the priest.
With God's blessing we deliver this bomb.

MAN

Two hundred miles ahead the weather plane
circled our target. We heard its message –
cloud cover less than three-tenths.
At the appointed time we began our ascent.

CHORUS

Our God is manly! In war he refuses us nothing!

MAN

The city below, its river and its tributaries
resembled an outstretched hand.
We shed our burden, our heavy burden,
and turned for home.

CHORUS

Refuses us nothing. Nothing. Nothing.

Four

MAN
Our minds are clear of all emotion.

CHORUS
Pure thought alone describes the universe.

MAN
Freely elected, chosen by the people,
we are the makers of laws.

CHORUS
Diligent, logical, disciplined men.

MAN
In our sure hands the security of the State.

CHORUS
The defence of order, freedom, property,
sovereignty, the aspirations of the people.

MAN
Whom we serve.

CHORUS
Whom we lead.

MAN
Secrecy is essential when decisions
weigh heavy on the men of State.
The weak-hearted, the effeminate, the disloyal
must know nothing.

CHORUS
The juries are pricked, the rule of law prevails.

MAN
The enemy incites the traitors in our midst.

CHORUS
Dissidents, extremists, beware!
The rule of law prevails!

Five

WOMAN
All night I searched for my daughter.
At dawn a neighbour told me
she had seen her by the river,
among the dead and dying.

I heard her voice calling Mother, Mother,
and I went towards the sound.
My child was completely burned.
The skin had come off her head,
leaving a knot of twisted hair.

My daughter said, Mother, you're late, so late,
please take me back. It hurts, it hurts.
Please take me home. But there were no homes,
no doctors, there was nothing I could do.

I covered up her naked body and held her
in my arms for seven hours.
Late at night she cried out again, Mother,
Mother, and put her arm around my neck,
her small cold arm.

I said, Please say Mother again.
But that was the last time.

CHORUS
When the stars threw down their spears,
And water'd heaven with their tears,
Did He smile His work to see?
Did He who made the Lamb make thee?

Six

MAN

Two great nations marshal their allies
and prepare for war. Two great nations,
born of revolutions, of compassionate visions
of a world made new, made good
in freedom and in justice.
Not granted by God to Kings,
but made afresh by men.

WOMAN

Is the world redeemed
by shifts of power among the men?

MAN

Here one nation stands jailer to its people's minds,
here the other ransacks the globe, a freedom
sustained by greed. The names of Lenin and Jefferson
are mouthed, the visions are forgotten.
The State appoints its enemies,
bureaucracies propound its simple lies.
The allies, fawning or coerced, take sides.
The cult of weaponry taints every mind,
derides compassion, distorts all relation.

War is urged by governments in the name of the people.

WOMAN

Shall we always be fooled by these ancient lies?
Who is my enemy? Who is the enemy of my child?

CHORUS

We shall crush you lest we shall be crushed.

Seven

Midsummer . . . two hours before dawn,
in the house below my husband and daughter sleep.
The stars fade, the moon has risen,
derided womanly moon who longs to be
our emblem in this manly world.

Grieving moon, do our virile times
suggest to you the metaphor of rape,
the conquest of nature, the slaughter of species,
the burning of forests, the poisoning of ocean and air,
the tyranny of scale, the weapons, the weapons.

MAN AND WOMAN
Our science mocks magic and the human heart,
our knowledge is the brutal mastery of the unknown.

CHORUS
Cruelty has a human heart,
And jealousy a human face;
Terror the human form divine,
And secrecy the human dress.

The human dress is forged iron,
The human form a fiery forge,
The human face a furnace sealed,
The human heart its hungry gorge.

WOMAN
Shall there be womanly times, or shall we die?
Are there men unafraid of gentleness?

Can we have strength without aggression,
without disgust,
strength to bind feeling to the intellect?

MAN AND WOMAN
The planet does not turn for us alone.
Science is a form of wonder, knowledge a form of love.
Are we too late to love ourselves?
Shall we change, or shall we die?

WOMAN
The moon lifts higher and brightens.
Only shadows point the way.

CHORUS
For Mercy has a human heart,
Pity a human face,
And Love, the human form divine,
And Peace, the human dress.

Then every man, of every clime,
That prays in his distress,
Prays to the human form divine,
Love, Mercy, Pity, Peace.

The
Ploughman's
Lunch

Introduction

Early in 1981 I had some preliminary conversations with
Richard Eyre about the kind of film we wanted to make.
For me at any rate, our notions were usefully vague. Our film
was to be set in the present and to be somehow 'about' the
present. We wanted the textures of everyday London – the
Underground, Brixton High Street – stylishly done. We
hoped Jonathan Pryce would play an important role. I had
read and admired E. P. Thompson's collection of essays,
Reading by Candlelight and Milan Kundera's novel, *The Book
of Laughter and Forgetting*. I thought our subject might
encompass the uses we make of the past, and the dangers, to
an individual as well as to a nation, of living without a sense
of history. We had been impressed by Wajda's film, *Man of
Iron*, especially by the pathetic, sweaty alcoholic at its centre.

I gave myself a year to research and write the film, a leisurely
schedule by film standards. In a twelve-year-old notebook I
came across a reference to an item on *Woman's Hour* which
described how the pub snack, the ploughman's lunch, was
not an English tradition but an invention of an advertising
campaign mounted to persuade people to eat in pubs. *The
Ploughman's Lunch* became a working title and then,
imperceptibly, a controlling metaphor for self-serving
fabrications of the past. For many months I thought the film's
action would take place against the background of the Royal
Family and the pressmen who follow it about. But by the end

of the summer and the Royal Wedding, I was wearying and finding it difficult to maintain a keen anthropological interest in the subject.

About this time I asked to spend a day watching the television news being made and through a benign error found myself in the BBC radio newsroom. The BBC news, at least the solemn Radio Three and Four versions, is about the closest we have to an official version of events. It carries great authority. And yet the newsroom itself, with its dusty spider plants and well-established rituals, resembled the cosy staffroom of an old grammar school; the early morning news briefings were like school assemblies, wearily conducted, dutifully attended. It seemed to me a perfect setting.

To a generation the Suez crisis of 1956 appeared to speed the collapse of the idea – by that time an illusion anyway – of Britain as a world power. The government of the day had acted deceitfully while trying to appear virtuous. Our subservient role to the Americans was dramatized, and the crisis initiated a long period of national introspection. I had my own reasons for wanting to write about Suez. I was eight years old at the time of the invasion and living in Libya where my father was an officer in the British Army. Anti-British feeling was naturally strong among the Libyans and Army families were herded into armed camps for protection. My mother happened to be in England at the time, and for some weeks I lived in a tent with other children not so very far from a machine-gun nest. My father was a remote, organizing figure with a service revolver strapped around his waist. Suddenly everyday routines belonged to a distant past and I understood for the first time that political events were real and affected people's lives – they were not just stories in the papers that grown-ups read.

In 1981, with the liberal consensus and political idealism generally in retreat, it seemed plausible to imagine how an ambitious writer might set out to rewrite the Crisis in terms of the steely pragmatism being promoted now by the government of Mrs Thatcher. The past would be re-interpreted while the amateur historian unconsciously acted out in his private life a sequence of betrayals and deceits which would parallel the events he was distorting in his history.

I watched television commercials being made and attended the Labour and Conservative Party Conferences. By this time it was clear that the main characters of *The Ploughman's Lunch* were all involved professionally in shaping our concepts of ourselves as citizens and as a nation. These principal characters were an editor, a journalist, a television researcher, a commercials director and a historian.

By the time I gave Richard Eyre the first draft of the script in March 1982 the Falklands affair was beginning to unfold. The Fleet set sail while we were still tinkering with our second draft. The Falklands War was not, of course, a re-run of the Suez crisis. The Egyptians had a legitimate claim on the canal that runs through their territory, while the Argentinians had little more than an emotional claim on the Falkland Islands. However, the connections between the two events were striking. A large task force was to be despatched and lives were to be risked to regain territory which successive British governments had been trying quietly to unload on the Argentinians. The Islanders themselves had consistently been denied full British citizenship. It was not clear then, and it is even less clear now, that the Government conducted negotiations in good faith to avoid armed conflict. The eruption of jingoism, the thunderous Churchillian rhetoric which was so readily available to politicians of all persuasions showed that this was less a matter of real territorial ambition, or a desire to protect 'our own'; but, like Suez, more an affair of the heart, of who we thought we were, who we wanted to be.

The Falklands War gave James Penfield a clearer motive for wanting to re-write Suez. At last we were acting independently of the Americans, we had 'found ourselves' and it was time to undo the embarrassment and breast-beating that attached itself to 1956. I made small adjustments to the script to keep the Falklands quietly and steadily in the background. There were some odd surprises. In the first draft a reference is made to the resignation of an imaginary Foreign Secretary. By the second draft, a real Foreign Secretary had resigned. In the first draft the historian, Ann Barrington, mentions how her late husband fought to preserve the BBC's independence during the Suez crisis. By the time I was writing a second draft the BBC was under attack once more and she is able to comment that 'he would be useful to them now'.

More important changes, however, came at the instigation of the director. When Richard Eyre asked to know more about James Penfield's background, I added the visit home, his refusals over the phone to return to his mother's deathbed, his denial in front of Susan, the girl he is pursuing, that his parents are alive and the funeral scene at the end when Penfield glances at his watch. While government Ministers responded painstakingly to the demands of the script that they deliver in their speeches 'invocations of nationhood and historical mission', it was Richard who gave the Conference scenes their narrative as well as visual coherence. In many other ways he suggested or prompted changes, not in order to put his own directorial stamp on the material, but, generously, to enable me to articulate more clearly what was already there.

In *The Ploughman's Lunch* most of the characters are
unpleasant – though I do like to think they have a certain
residual charm. They start out bad, and get worse. Among
those whose job it is to pretend to know what the cinema-
going public wants, there is a widespread assumption that
audiences must have characters with whom they can
'identify'. Serious novelists and playwrights may find this
insistence quaint; moral values can be as easily, if not more
plausibly, embodied in a narrative structure as in any right-
thinking or suddenly reformed character. This nursery tale
aesthetic ('but where's the good guy?') pervades mainstream
cinema investment and it has been left to film makers
working with small budgets raised with extraordinary difficulty
to demonstrate over and over again that there is a sophisticated
and commercially significant cinema audience looking for
more than mere escape.

During the editing of the film, a number of changes were
made to the order of the scenes. What appears to be a
satisfactory narrative sequence in script form often needs
rethinking once the scenes are shot. I have kept to our final
edited version here. In a number of places I have retained
lines or parts of lines that were lost during filming or editing,
but mostly I have followed the post-production script.

The name of Channel Four appears nowhere in the credits
and it therefore seems right to end by saying that it provided
a substantial part of the budget. Without this participation it
is unlikely that we could have made the film.

Oxford 1985

The Ploughman's Lunch was produced by Simon Relph and Ann Scott and was made entirely on location in London, Brighton and Norfolk by Greenpoint Films Limited. It went on general release in Great Britain in 1983 and in the United States of America in 1984. The cast was as follows:

JAMES PENFIELD	Jonathan Pryce
JOURNALISTS	William Maxwell/
	Paul Jesson/
	Andy Rashleigh
YOUNG JOURNALIST	Christopher Fulford
NEWSREADER	David Lyon
GOLD	David de Keyser
GOLD'S ASSISTANT	Polly Abbott
JEREMY HANCOCK	Tim Curry
SUSAN BARRINGTON	Charlie Dore
BOB TUCKETT	Peter Walmsley
EDITOR	Bob Cartland
MR PENFIELD	Nat Jackley
MRS PENFIELD	Pearl Hackney
EDWARD	Simon Stokes
WOMAN AT POETRY READING	Anna Wing
YOUNG MAN AT POETRY READING	Ken Drury
STUDENT AT POETRY READING	Richard Cottan
BARMAN	Peter Birch
LECTURER	Bill Paterson
SQUASH COACH	Ken Shorter
TOM FOX	Orlando Wells
ANN BARRINGTON	Rosemary Harris
MATTHEW FOX	Frank Finlay
JACEK	Witold Schejbal
BETTY	Libba Davies
CARMEN	Sandra Voe
PETE	Andrew Norton

CAROL	Cecily Hobbs
JILL	Clare Sutcliffe
DAD IN COMMERCIAL	Robert McIntosh
MUM IN COMMERCIAL	Vivienne Chandler
DAUGHTER IN COMMERCIAL	Nicole Kleeman
SON IN COMMERCIAL	Bernard Mullims
JUNIOR MINISTER	Allan Mitchell

Technical credits

Director	RICHARD EYRE
Production Manager	REDMOND MORRIS
Sound Mixer	DAVID STEPHENSON
Casting Director	SUSIE FIGGIS
Assistant Director	SIMON RELPH
Continuity	PAT RAMBAUT
Art Director	MICHAEL PICKWOAD
Construction Manager	JOHN HEDGES
Prop Buyer	TRISHA EDWARDS
Prop Master	ROY CANNON
Costumes designed by	LUCIANA ARRIGHI
Associate Costume designer	JOY KLEINER
Wardrobe Mistress	RITA WAKELY
Make-up	ELAINE CAREW
Hairdresser	JOAN CARPENTER
Accountant	ALAN JOHN
Dubbing Editor	RICHARD DUNFORD
Dubbing Mixer	GERRY HUMPHRIES
Music Recordist	JOHN RICHARDS
2nd Assistant Directors	CHRISTOPHER FIGG/ LINDA BRUCE
Production Assistant	RACHEL NEALE
Assistant Accountant	DEBORAH BARNARD
Production Runner	JASPER FFORDE
Focus Puller	DAVID BRYANT
Clapper-Loaders	SUE GIBSON/JEREMY HILES
Camera Grip	TED WHITBY

Camera Car Driver	NODDY WOODWARD
Boom Operator	KEITH PAMPLIN
Sound Engineer	DESMOND EDWARDS
Assistant Editors	MICHAEL PARKINSON/SIMON HARRIS
Publicity	DEREK ROBBINS
Stills Photographer	JOHN BROWN
Special Photography	JOHN HAYNES
Casting Assistant	LEONORA DAVIS
Standby Props	JOHN HEMMINGTON/PAUL TURLEY
Dressing Prop	REG WHEELER
Standbys	CYRIL FITZWALTER/TIM HAYES/ RAY JONES/DANNY HUOHY
Gaffer	TOM BROWN
Electricians	STEVE MCLEOD/BILL MERRELL/ BILL THORNHILL
Construction	REG RICHARDS/BILL MCARTHY/ ROY O'CONNA
Transport	GEOFF HUGHES/MICHAEL GREEN/ NORMAN BANNER/ FRANK BARRETTA
Camera and Lenses by	JOE DUNTON CAMERAS LIMITED
Processed by	RANK FILM LABORATORIES
Lighting by	LEE ELECTRIC (LIGHTING) LIMITED
Title design by	NICHOLAS JENKINS
Music recorded at	CTS STUDIOS LIMITED
Caterers	J&J CATERING LIMITED
Miss Dore's cocktail dress by	ZAI
Post-production services at	MERCURY CUTTING ROOMS TWICKENHAM FILM STUDIOS

Thanks to Christopher Reid for Edward's poem, Christopher Hitchens, Francis Wheen, and The Women's Peace Camp, Greenham Common

1 BBC radio newsroom, late morning

We are in close as a story arrives on a press service teleprinter. A hand tears away the sheet. The camera tracks as we follow the story. It passes through the copytaster's hands and is passed on down the room to the summaries desk.

This is a time of steady activity. Journalists move about the room to consult. Others are writing in longhand, and several are dictating copy to typists who are all women. One or two people – newsreaders – sit about doing nothing. Much movement of paper.

Over the sound of typewriters and the murmur of dictating voices we hear a woman's voice over the PA announce, 'The Leader of the Opposition on five'. A few journalists pick up headsets, but they do not stop writing. We establish the atmosphere – laconic but efficient, and a little down-at-heel.

At the summaries desk we find James Penfield. He stands to the side of and a little behind a seated secretary, dictating in a laconic deadpan voice from a sheet of scrawled longhand.

JAMES Between fifty and sixty scrap metal workers are . . .

The phone rings. James snatches it up and answers without breaking stride.

Hello. Newsroom.

The secretary waits, her face totally inexpressive.

Who? Paul Dean? He doesn't work here anymore.

ANOTHER JOURNALIST (*calling over his shoulder as he passes*). Went to IRN.

JAMES No. No. Sorry. Try IRN.

He drops the receiver and continues. The secretary reactivates.

. . . reported to have landed illegally on the island of South Georgia in the South Atlantic. The Foreign Office reacted sceptically to reports that the Argentine Government was planning . . .

2 Newsroom, late morning

James and a newsreader (one of those we saw earlier doing nothing) stand together by the photocopier. Walking with controlled haste and carrying the news-sheets, they head towards the studio. A clock behind them shows two minutes to twelve.

3 Studio, late morning

James and the newsreader sit at a table in the studio, fairly close together. The newsreader settles himself behind the microphone. James sits back, professionally bored, rolling a stub of a pencil between his fingers.

Through a large loudspeaker we hear a Radio 4 programme winding up. Theme music.

The newsreader has a plummy, authoritative voice and is a year or two younger than James. He stares down at his news sheet.

From the Control Room a woman announces 'One Minute'.

JAMES How's Mary?

NEWSREADER (*stung, then recovering*). Oh, she's well. Jolly well. Thanks. Very well indeed.

From the Studio Controller's point of view we see the Newsroom behind James and the newsreader, who chat soundlessly.

WOMAN'S VOICE
Before the news at twelve o'clock, there's just time to tell you about Woman's Hour this afternoon. Commander Freddy Bracknell will be talking about his four years as a German POW in Stalag Three, and mountaineer John Clayton will be reliving the thrills and perils of Everest. Also, Polly Morrell will be finding out from the historian Professor John Gerty how the governments of Eastern Europe distort their recent past in history books to suit their present policies and allegiances. That's Freddy Bracknell, John Clayton and John Gerty, all on Woman's Hour just after two o'clock this afternoon.

The six pips. The sweep hand of the clock. The red light.

NEWSREADER BBC News at twelve o'clock. There is cautious optimism in Brussels that a formula may be reached to break—

4 Brixton, late afternoon

James hurries home through the din of rush-hour Brixton.

5 James's flat, late afternoon

James's flat is one floor of a large Victorian house. Two decent-sized rooms knocked together make a very large bedsitting room. Tiny kitchen and bathroom off. Bare boards, junk furniture, but elegant. Heavy stereo stack, a lot of records, a lot of paperbacks.

In high spirits, James prepares to go out. He chooses a shirt, begins to undress. The TV is on.

6 James's flat, night

An hour later. James is dressed to go out. The big room is now in darkness except for a light by James's armchair. He is talking on the phone to his friend Jeremy Hancock.

JAMES C'mon, you promised . . . tell her you've got to finish a piece . . . I know . . . I know, but it's my big night . . . yes she's going to *be* there . . . C'mon! All I want you to do is introduce me to her. And remember, build me up . . . good man.

7 Publishing house, night

A high-ceilinged room in a publishing house, Bloomsbury. A launch party. About forty guests. Waiters take round trays with glasses of wine. By some large double doors is a display of school textbooks. Most prominently featured is the book being launched today – Goldbooks Schools Series No. 5 The Cold War, edited by Professor J. Gerty.

James is led by a Personal Assistant through the crowd to meet Gold, who is surrounded by attentive young men.

GOLD . . . took him by the elbow, steered him into a quiet corner and said, 'Where do you think you are, young man? Fabers?'

From the circle polite laughter. Gold extends his hand towards James.

Glad you could come.

PERSONAL ASSISTANT James Penfield.

GOLD Good, good. Now, is someone getting you a drink?

PERSONAL ASSISTANT Wrote the Berlin Airlift chapter.

Job done, PA fades.

GOLD I know, I know! Gentlemen, let me introduce you to one of our most talented contributors to *The Cold War*. James Penfield. He wrote the opening chapter, on 'The Berlin Airlift'. One of the best chapters in the book.

JAMES Hello.

GOLD I won't introduce you all by name. Basically James, this is our UK sales team. What was I saying? Yes, these graduate trainees . . .

Twenty minutes later.

Jeremy has just come in and is surveying the room from the doorway. He takes a drink from a tray, notices James across the room and smiles ruefully.

Jeremy Hancock is a journalist, same age as James, good-looking and well-dressed. A faintly corrupt look about him, despite this. He is intelligent and intensely self-regarding.

James makes his way through the crowd towards Jeremy. They stand in the doorway – a position which affords them a good view of the guests in the room and of those guests who are still arriving by way of a grand and ornate stairway.

JEREMY My dear James.

With mock solemnity, he kisses James on the cheek.

JAMES Not here.

JEREMY To the airlift.

JAMES The airlift.

JEREMY Any sign of the goddess Barrington?

JAMES Not yet. Do you know any of these people?

JEREMY One or two. A grey lot. Some social democrats. Some diligent anti-communists. A political section man from the US Embassy. And this exquisite Californian wine, courtesy of the CIA.

JAMES Nonsense.

They look across the room at Gold being listened to.

JEREMY By the way, I hear that your Mr Gold is about to become very rich. I hope you told him that most of the ideas in your Berlin airlift chapter came from me.

JAMES Fuck off.

SUSAN (*off*). So it's all worked out perfectly . . .

JAMES That's her.

The two men go to the head of the stairs to watch Susan come up.

SUSAN She gets the house, he gets the cars. And the baby is still in Switzerland with the au pair.

Susan Barrington is in her late twenties. Flamboyant, effortlessly confident, she inhabits that special world – with its different rules – of the truly ambitious. James's fascination owes as much to the certainties of her class as to her looks.

An attentive young man accompanies her up the stairs.

Jeremy makes a sound. Susan glances up.

SUSAN Jeremy!

She waves and her elbow catches a tray of champagne being carried downstairs. Glasses fall about her feet. While apologizing, Susan does not take her eyes off Jeremy.

SUSAN How stupid! I am sorry.

The butler and the young man drop to the ground and set about picking up the glasses. Susan regards them for a moment, then steps round them and hurries up the stairs.

Jeremy and Susan go into a clinch, with kisses. James stands a few feet off.

Jeremy! How fantastic.

JEREMY Darling Susan.

SUSAN You're so famous now.

JEREMY And you're so beautiful. What are you doing here?

SUSAN We're thinking of doing this current affairs thing for schools. World history since 1945. Twelve programmes, lots of stock film.

JEREMY In that case, you should meet my very dear friend, James Penfield. Brilliant analyst of recent history, and a world authority on the Berlin Airlift.

James and Susan say 'Hi' and shake hands.

SUSAN Was that your chapter, then? It was very good.

JAMES Thank you. We met last week, at the Wajda film. You won't remember. We didn't actually speak.

SUSAN (*not remembering*). Yes, that's right. And look, I'm being terribly rude. Bob? Oh, Bob. This is Bob Tuckett. Bob was at Oxford too.

Bob, Jeremy, James all say 'Hi'. Momentarily enthusiasm flags, no one speaks. Then the drinks tray is suddenly in their midst and they all reach out thankfully, with mock groans of relief and surprise.

An hour later. Guests are leaving. James has got Susan alone. They descend the stairs. Close in on Susan. A desperate kind of seriousness.

I mean, in many ways I'm right behind the women's movement. But sometimes I wish they'd get on with it instead of moaning on. The office was split right down the middle. I mean, as a *woman* I understood what they were saying, that current affairs was all about what men did, but as a human *being* and a *television* researcher, as a *professional*, I could just sense they'd got it all wrong. I could see there were two paths I could go down, power or not-power. Down the not-power path was lots of sisterly feeling, masochism and frustration. Down the other path, I could keep on working. So of course I voted with the men and the other women all resigned. I think they're mad, don't you?

They arrive by the front door. There is the briefest pause. James makes his bid.

JAMES Can I give you a lift?

SUSAN No, it's all right. I can get a cab. Night night.

James stands in the doorway and watches her go.

8 Oxford Circus, day

An abrupt transition. Morning rush hour, Brixton Underground station to Oxford Circus. James fights his way through the crowd up the Underground steps leading to the street. He is late.

9 Langham Place, day

James runs away from the camera towards Broadcasting House.

10 News Conference Room, day

Same time. Moulded plastic chairs are ranged along the walls of the room. Some journalists stand, some are half asleep. The feel of a morning assembly.

*Seated at the only desk, by the door, sits the Editor-in-Chief.
While waiting he pretends to look at papers.*

The tone of these meetings is restrained, weary.

*The Editor speaks with short pauses between each point.
Quietly, as though talking to himself.*

EDITOR Use of this word 'finally'. We've had this one before.
Difficult when it gets . . .

*James comes in. The Editor ignores him pointedly. There are
no more seats. James stands somewhere inconspicuous.*

. . . when it gets too close to 'finally the main points of the
news' . . . Now today. Not a very sexy list. We can't live off
all these court cases . . . Royals . . . What's Charles giving
Diana for her birthday?

1ST JOURNALIST He's not telling.

EDITOR Better follow him around, I suppose.

2ND JOURNALIST Newcastle is following Charles to see if
anyone throws a bottle at his car like last time.

EDITOR Good . . . Now, I'm going to drop this panda business
unless something happens soon.

2ND JOURNALIST We've got two people down at the zoo
looking into the cage.

EDITOR Give it one more day. These scrap-iron merchants on,
where is it, Gritviken? Anything in that?

JAMES Could be.

EDITOR Let's keep an eye on it then. OK, I'm just thinking
aloud. Let's take the list in order. *Cabinet reshuffle.* Chris?

1ST JOURNALIST Bob is ringing round the ministries finding out where everyone is going to be. That'll come to fruition later this morning. John'll be at Caxton Hall. We'll try and lay on a radio car.

Through this last speech we close in on James. Behind his news prospects sheet he is reading a letter. We glimpse the letter heading: 'Goldbooks'.

EDITOR Prime Minister is on the Jimmy Young Show at ten-thirty. We should get something out of that. Now, matters Irish . . .

11 James's flat, evening

James is clearing a desk he has against a wall, in preparation for work on his Suez book. It is a desk that has not seen much use before, piled high with clutter. He brings over a lamp for it, arranges the typewriter in its centre. Various London library books are arranged along one edge.

On the wall above the desk, James pins a large map of Europe and the Mediterranean. He sits at the desk, lines up a couple of pencils . . . and picks up a book.

12 Restaurant, day

Langan's, Piccadilly. Gold and James are met at the door by the head waiter. Gold is obviously known here. Businessmen, media people, agents, conspiracy, urgency, babble.

Cornucopia too – dessert trolley, cheese trolley, something being flambée'd *at a table. Another shot through the diners and we find Gold and James already seated. The main course has been cleared away. A clock shows the time to be ten to three.*

JAMES I was only ten years old at the time, but it was the first international crisis I can remember. It's obviously a key point in our recent history, *the* key point, and I've always thought that sooner or later we would have re-examined Suez in the light of subsequent events. And now, suddenly, with this Falklands business on us, it's quite clear we do need to take another look at 1956. The way I see the book is that it would get away completely—

The waiter has wheeled up the dessert trolley. Gold has been examining it for the last few seconds before breaking in.

GOLD Would you like a dessert . . . I'm having one.

JAMES No thanks. I'd like to break away—

GOLD I'll have some of that.

JAMES . . . break away completely from—

GOLD And some of that. Sorry.

JAMES . . . from all the moralizing and talk of national humiliation that is now the standard line on Suez . . .

Gold has a great forkful of gâteau near his face.

GOLD Yes . . . you're not a socialist then.

JAMES No. I'd want to—

GOLD Good.

JAMES I'd want to set out the events as they happened. The

way I'd see it is this: the British Empire was an ideal. It may have become totally obsolete by the middle of this century, but it wasn't totally dishonourable to try and defend its remains and try and salvage some self-respect, which is what I think the Conservatives were trying to do. Then there's the essential—

GOLD Are you going to have coffee?

JAMES Yes, please.

GOLD And you'll join me in a sambucca?

JAMES Thank you.

Gold speaks to the waiter as James continues.

. . . there's the business of the British collusion with Israel. Of course it's proved beyond all doubt now, but I'd want to set it in the context of diplomacy and warfare. I mean, if you're about to attack one country, it makes sense to encourage neighbouring countries to attack it too. The French understood this. They could never . . .

The waiter brings the coffee. Gold is lighting a cigar, having offered one to James.

The French could never make out all the embarrassment and breast-beating of the British. My enemy's enemy is my friend. It's as simple as that. If we had not been so scrupulous, we would not have been so ashamed.

The waiter brings the sambuccas. We close-in on the drinks as James goes on talking. Gold puts a match to James's drink on this next line.

Now it's as if we've discovered ourselves again. We're acting independently when the standard line has always been that after Suez we couldn't lift a finger without the Americans . . .

13 Arcade, day.

Gold and James stroll through the arcade, bloated from their lunch. Both are slightly drunk. Gold is expansive.

GOLD Personally James, I'm very excited by this new arrangement we have. It gives us direct access to literally hundreds of American colleges. Twentieth-century history is a growth area over there, don't ask me why. Your readership will be first and second year American college students . . .

JAMES Freshmen and sophomores . . .

GOLD You know the lingo. Jolly good. So your language will have to be simple, not stupid, mind, but simple, very, very simple, and always remember it's an American readership.

JAMES Like I was saying, the American angle in Suez is very important. I wouldn't want to say they let us down. I think that's wrong. A good ally is one who doesn't back you up in your mistakes, who tells you when to pull back. And the Americans were good allies. Simple as that.

James is immensely pleased with his own performance during this speech. Gold, however, is more interested in something he has seen in a shop window. As soon as James finishes, Gold mumbles an apology and plunges into the shop. James follows him in.

14 Newsroom, day

A lull in the action. Most of the journalists are eating out. A few eat sandwiches, smoke, chat, read. A background television shows crowd scenes from Argentina.

James sits with a plastic cup of coffee reading intently.

He stands at the window looking out over the roofs. Then he turns abruptly, picks up a telephone and dials.

JAMES Is that London Midweek? . . . Susan Barrington.

15 A suburban street, north-west London, day

James turns off the street up the front path of a nondescript pre-war semi.

16 James's parents' house, day

Mr Penfield comes into the hall to answer the door. He is a tired-looking man in his sixties. James enters. The two men fumble awkwardly between a handshake and an embrace. It is James who favours the former.

MR PENFIELD Hello, Jimmy.

JAMES Dad.

MR PENFIELD Come into the kithchen. I'm just making your mother's tea.

17 Kitchen, day

Mr Penfield fusses inexpertly at the stove. James leans in the doorway.

JAMES So how is she?

MR PENFIELD Well, she doesn't complain much. You know what she's like. She keeps asking when you're coming . . .

JAMES I'm sorry about Saturday, Dad. It was just impossible to get away.

MR PENFIELD Oh, she knows you're very busy, especially now, with everything going on . . . the doctor said to try her on solids, but she's been right off her food . . . You take this up to her. Tell her you made it. She'll like that.

James picks up the tray – tinned tomato soup, buttered bread, and a cup of tea.

18 Bedroom, day

Mrs Penfield lies on her back, dozing. She is plainly very ill. James sits at the bedside. The tray of food cools on a bedside table. We have a sense of time passing.

Mrs Penfield opens her eyes. James kisses her on the cheeks.

MRS PENFIELD Jimmy. I knew you'd come today. I said to Dad this morning, that boy'll be here this afternoon, just you see. He said don't get your hopes up, but I knew . . .

This speech appears to exhaust her. Her eyes close. She keeps hold of James's hand. She murmers

Have you got to go straight off?

JAMES No, not yet.

MRS PENFIELD Good . . . stay here a bit.

James sits. His mother falls into a deep sleep.

19 Living-room, evening

Mr Penfield sits drinking tea and watching TV. He stands when James enters and turns the set off.

JAMES She's asleep.

Mr Penfield indicates a seat to James.

MR PENFIELD Everyone's been marvellous really, Jimmy. The neighbours come and sit with her while I'm at work.

JAMES That's good.

MR PENFIELD And Joe Ramage – you remember him – he comes and helps me out in the shop.

JAMES Yes, you said.

MR PENFIELD Now, are you going to have some more tea?

JAMES No, thanks Dad.

MR PENFIELD Or a beer. I've got some in.

James shakes his head. There is a long awkward silence, a hopeless silence that it is particular to both father and son. Finally James gets to his feet.

JAMES I've got to be going. I've got a meeting tonight.

MR PENFIELD The bed's all made up if you want to stay.

JAMES I'll ring you in the next couple of days.
Mr Penfield stands, and nods. This is a familiar exchange. Finish on him.

20 Barbican Arts Complex, afternoon

James and Susan arrive at the Barbican together. Their conversation is a little detached from its subject matter. They are feeling each other out. They are not disagreeing here. As they talk they make a complicated route through the Arts Centre, always on the verge of getting lost.

JAMES What did you think of that Wajda film?

SUSAN I *quite* liked it. I wasn't as enthusiastic as everyone else was.

JAMES I thought it was tremendous.

SUSAN I think it went on rather too long.

JAMES I couldn't bear for it to end.

SUSAN And I didn't like that man.

JAMES Oh, but he was terrific.

SUSAN And the shape of it all. It was sort of . . . shapeless.

JAMES Really? I thought those long flashbacks were extremely good.

SUSAN I know what you mean. But I don't like flashbacks. They make me feel as though I'm holding my breath. I like progress.

21 Lift, afternoon

JAMES You don't like flashbacks because your mother's a historian.

SUSAN Good theory. But I like my mother. I have no aversions to what she does.

JAMES Too bad. What did your father do?

SUSAN My real father? Well, he was a flashback.

They laugh as they step out of the lift.

22 Barbican Art Gallery, late afternoon

A little later. A Private View. *A discreetly murmuring crowd, wine, canapés.*

The paintings – painfully pretentious – represent various forms of aesthetic self-consciousness.

James and Susan look at the pictures, but make no reference to them. They spend a little time in front of each one before moving to the next. James's speech is broken by moments of contemplation. As they move on again, he picks up his thread.

JAMES Everyone describes the same process. At first it *is* exciting. You're at the centre of the world. As soon as anything happens, you're among the first to know about it. And there are deadlines a dozen times a day, even more, and that's intimidating and exciting. Then you get the hang of it and the excitement wears off. You're a clerk in a rather dowdy office. There's none of the glamour of television, or the penetration of serious journalism. You're a processor of semi-official news. Some people leave at this stage. Then, if you hang on, and especially if you're promoted, you discover a new kind of pleasure. You're pleased by the ease with which you can write summaries and bulletins from news agency printouts, by the way you can judge length. Ending a broadcast on the dot, having everything run smoothly, selecting a running order that makes sense, knowing instinctively what you can and cannot do. Professionalism.

SUSAN And you're at this third stage.

JAMES No, there's a fourth. Numbness. You do everything right, but you feel nothing either way.

SUSAN I think you're exaggerating. And if you aren't, you should jolly well change your job.

JAMES Oh yes?

SUSAN Yes. You're much too old to be making a drama out of alienation, or whatever you call it. You've got to take responsibility for your own happiness. That's what I think, anyway.

Susan has moved on a couple of steps and is bending forwards to look at a picture. James smiles at her wonderingly, a little deflated, but impressed.

23 James's flat, evening

Jeremy is sprawled in a chair with a drink. James is standing.
Muted piano music from the stereo. Edward has just entered.
The other two have been waiting for him.

JAMES It's the Poet Laureate himself.

Edward approaches. He is a contemporary of the other two,
but looks much younger and less worldly in manner. He is
slightly nervous. He works on a literary magazine and he is a
poet whose work is just beginning to be recognized.
The three are old friends. Jeremy and James keep up their
friendship with Edward because they recognize his talent, and
this makes them feel more authentic. Edward keeps up with
them because he is lonely and his own life is rather dull.
However, he does distrust them a little. And they keep his talent
in place by teasing him.

As Edward enters the other two applaud.

JEREMY How sweet.

Edward makes a nervous mock bow.

EDWARD Thank you. Have you two been smoking that illegal
stuff again?

James pours wine into Edward's glass.

JAMES We were just admiring your poem in the TLS, Edward.

EDWARD Ah, yes.

JEREMY It's terribly good.

EDWARD Don't tell me you've actually read it, Jeremy.

James picks up the TLS and waves it at Edward.

JEREMY Committed to memory. Forever.

EDWARD I see.

JAMES Blasé and epicene.

JEREMY We were just chortling over that. Blasé and epicene.
It perfectly describes the new Foreign Secretary. So – I hope
you won't mind, Edward, I pinched it for my piece today.

EDWARD Attributed?

JEREMY Of course.

EDWARD Why, is there a new Foreign Secretary? Who was
the old one anyway?

JEREMY It needn't concern you, Edward. James has got some
news. He needs a poet's advice.

Jeremy pats a seat. Edward sits down.

JAMES C'mon. I don't want any jokes about this.

JEREMY No jokes. James is in love.

EDWARD Congratulations. Who with?

JEREMY A glamorous young lady way above his station . . .

JAMES Bastard.

JEREMY Name of Susie Barrington. Daughter of the eminent
historian, Ann Barrington, step-daughter of scandalous
Matthew Byrd the acclaimed sack-artist . . .

Lay over Jeremy's account on next scene and fade down slowly.

24 Susan's flat, late evening

A sumptuously cluttered place. A chesterfield. Deep armchairs, silk cushions, many prints, coffee table, books. Clearly an inherited place.

Susan is pouring coffee. James sits across from her, jacket off, sunk in cushions.

Jeremy's voice-over recedes.

SUSAN Mummy and I – we were more like lovers, really, or sisters. Then a couple of years after Daddy died, and not long after I left Oxford, she started seeing various men and I was furious. I really was upset. I stopped going home, I never phoned. I went round telling everyone how awful her books were. And she hardly seemed to notice, and that made me angrier. Then I got a job I was interested in, and *I* started to see lots of different men, and I suppose I grew up a little and began to understand. So I wrote her a long letter, almost *seven* pages, saying how sorry I was, and how I was worried that we were drifting apart. And do you know,

(A pause.)

she wrote me a poem, a really beautiful poem about mothers and daughters.

JAMES How nice.

SUSAN It makes me weepy just to remember it. So we were fine again, and then she got married to Matthew who's a womanizer and a bit of a yob, but quite nice really, makes TV commercials. What about yours?

JAMES Both dead.

SUSAN That must be rather nice, in a way. I mean, you don't have any . . .

The door bell rings loudly.

Damn. They're early.

JAMES Who?

SUSAN I called you a taxi.

JAMES Very thoughtful.

SUSAN (*a gesture of helplessness*).
Well, you know . . .

25 Front door, Susan's flat, late evening

A minute later. James and Susan stands at the front door. Portico and steps down to street. Taxi waits. They kiss. Susan draws back.

JAMES Again?

SUSAN Yes, if you like. Call me at work.

James descends the stairs. Susan closes the door.

26 Cocktail bar, early evening

A cocktail bar, a self-conscious imitation of the American model. James and Jeremy sit on high stools at the bar. Tall, colourful drinks are just being set down in front of them. On a TV there are scenes of the departing Royal Navy fleet.

JEREMY To the Fleet.

JAMES To the Fleet.

JEREMY And the Argies.

JAMES The Argies.

Jeremy reaches into his inside pocket and pulls out an envelope.

JEREMY Now, top secret file.

JAMES (*reaching for it*). Come on. Hand over.

Jeremy puts the envelope out of James's reach.

JEREMY Uh-huh. Tell me what you think of this first.

JAMES It's shit.

JEREMY You approve!

JAMES Let me see.

JEREMY Get away. You'll see when I'm ready. First I want you to reflect on my noble behaviour, on how your interests are closest to my heart, how I lay awake at night worrying . . .

JAMES Jeremy, just let me see what you've got.

JEREMY You're so hard. All right then. I was chatting to some people from the diary page, and the name of Barrington came up. I expressed an interest . . .

JAMES Oh yes . . .

JEREMY . . . an innocent interest, and found out that last year *Vogue* ran a series called 'Mothers and Daughters'. Number seven, Ann and Susan Barrington. Being a decent, loving friend I went to the files and made a copy for you.

JAMES Let me see.

JEREMY Ah, ah. There's more. The piece celebrates the undying affection between the eminent left-wing historian and her dazzling daughter. Then the news editor, who happened to be in the room, said that years ago, when he worked on *The Guardian*, Ann Barrington had written a very good piece on . . . guess . . . Suez. It was 1966, the tenth anniversary.

Jeremy hands over an envelope which James now opens.

She's never written a book on it, but she clearly knew a lot.

JAMES Mmm . . .

JEREMY It's obvious what you have to do. Your way into the daughter's pants is through the mother, up the Suez Canal . . .

JAMES You're so gross.

JEREMY She's very nice, apparently. Lives in Norfolk. And very left-wing. You'll have to watch yourself there.

JAMES Ha ha . . .

JEREMY According to this, the daughter goes up to stay quite often. You'll need to get yourself invited for the right weekend.

JAMES You've really got it all worked out, haven't you?

JEREMY No need to thank me, if you don't want to. Just pay for these drinks.

BARMAN That'll be eleven pounds, sir.

27 Polytechnic, day

James walks along a busy corridor in a polytechnic. In a recess to one side is a games room. Along the walls are Space Invader machines by the dozen. Students stand at the machines intently, their faces illuminated by the glow. We see some expertly handled Space Invader action. James approaches one of the players and asks directions. Without looking up the student points down the corridor.

28 Corridor, day

James stands outside the doors of a lecture hall. Inside a lecture is in progress. We catch a few words.

James pushes the door open.

29 Lecture hall, day

The lecturer glances back and acknowledges his presence.

James stands at the back of the hall for the end of the lecture.

LECTURER A vacuum had been created. If the United States did not fill it, it was assumed the Russians would.

Pause.

Next week I shall be considering the extent to which the behaviour of nation states or governments may be judged by the moral criteria we normally apply to individuals. Thank you.

The students stand and begin to move out. James and the lecturer move towards each other and shake hands.

30 Lecturer's room, day

James and the lecturer sit separated by a low table. A tape-recorder is on the lecturer's side of the table.

LECTURER Well, what you need to understand . . .

JAMES No, sorry, could you lean forward a bit when you speak.

LECTURER Oh. Is this all right? Um . . . you see, through the late summer and early autumn of 1956 the Egyptians were running the canal, *their* canal, that is, quite efficiently. Traffic was passing through unimpeded, for Nasser didn't want to provide the West with any reason for invading his country.

Is that loud enough, by the way?

JAMES It's OK.

LECTURER Right. So by the time the British and French launched their invasion at the beginning of November the main economic reasons for doing so had largely evaporated. What remained, especially for the British, were the more marginal and emotional arguments.

31 James's flat, evening

The lecturer's voice continues on the tape. James pours a drink as he listens and walks towards his desk.

LECTURER (*voice over*). Using the language of private behaviour you could say that this was an affair of the heart – the idea was to teach Nasser a lesson, to appear capable of acting independently, and to maintain face in the world, particularly the Arab world.

James switches the tape recorder off. He picks up the Vogue *'Mothers & Daughters' article and pins it to the map of Egypt.*

32 A community hall, evening

A poetry reading, given by Edward Long, has just come to an end. There are about fifty present, and empty chairs behind. Jeremy and James are in the audience.

Edward is reading the last stanza of a poem.

EDWARD And so the ferry moves
   across the bay,
Top heavy as a wedge of wedding
   cake,
Leaving us to return to our hotels.
Gulls in nautical trim cry their
   farewells,
Then drop with avaricious eyes to
   take
Souvenirs from the debris of the day.

He pauses.

Thank you very much.

There is earnest applause which peters out. Now, a tense silence.

Edward stares impassively at the audience until he catches the movement of half-raised arm.

Yes.

The questioner is a middle-class, middle-aged woman, rather twittery.

WOMAN Me?

EDWARD Yes.

WOMAN Oh, yes, well I thought I'd start the thing off by asking, you know, and you'll probably think it's a stupid question that you get all the time, but could you tell us a little of how you actually get ideas, I mean, your poems are quite extraordinary and beautiful and I wondered how they, well you know, came *about*.

*During this, Jeremy has caught James's eye and they have
started to giggle silently. This continues through the scene.
They hunch up and turn away from each other, shaking quietly,
half recover, become aware of each other, or of the absurdity
of the questions, or of Edward's attempts to deal with them,
and they fold up once more. From Edward's point of view
we see their heads duck down.*

EDWARD It isn't a stupid question, but it is a difficult one to
answer. I get ideas in much the same way as anyone does.
Perhaps the difference is that I take them more seriously. I
write them down – odd scraps of things. Then I seem to
know when I'm ready to start work on a poem. It takes shape
as I write it, very slowly.

While Edward answers, the woman nods vigorously.

*James and Jeremy recover in the brief pause between questions.
They lift tear-stained faces, then crack up at the next question.*

*A young man, anorak, flat autodidact's 'does-the-team-think'
voice. Piece of paper in hand, he stands, trembling.*

MAN You are one of the most praised poets of your generation
of younger poets, and the *Sunday Times* has called you a
cross between Dante and Philip Larkin. What is your reaction
to this?

EDWARD Well, it's silly really. (*Catching sight of Jeremy and
James.*) It's journalism. Yes?

A serious-looking student has his hand raised.

STUDENT Yes. What is the poet's role in society today?

*Close in on James, drawing breath. A sudden, sharp yelp from
Jeremy fighting for air. All heads turn. The two are almost
off their seats onto the floor. We close in on them and hear
their moans of 'No, no' and 'Stop, stop' and 'Sorry!'*

33 Newsroom, late morning

The newsroom. The teleprinters. The sheets arriving on the copytaster's desk. On the TV monitor there are pictures of the Fleet. On the PA a voice announces 'Edward Du Cann on Four'.

We find Philip standing by the bulletin desk. He is a graduate trainee, twenty-three years old. Earnest in manner, slightly ingratiating.

Immensely pleased with what he has just read, he moves towards the summaries desk with a piece of paper in each hand.

PHILIP James, look at this. At last.

James is standing by a secretary, dictating.

JAMES Wait . . . and with talks at the United Nations still making little progress, tension and anxiety settled on MPs of all parties in Westminster. Speaking on the Jimmy Young Show earlier today, Mrs Thatcher said the prospects of a peaceful solution did not look encouraging. What is it?

PHILIP Take a look at these.

James glances over the sheets.

JAMES Not bad.

PHILIP Fifteen news items. I got exactly the same running order as the bulletin desk. They're all old pros.

JAMES Terrific.

Philip moves on to show someone else nearby. We hear him explain his triumph again.

James makes a gesture and expression of contempt for the benefit of the seated secretaries.

A group of journalists passes through. James catches one of them by the arm.

JAMES Can I use the phone in your office?

JOURNALIST Sure.

34 Office, late morning

A small, bare office. A few minutes later. James is speaking on the phone to Susan.

JAMES You're being very elusive . . . tell them you're ill . . . or leave early then . . . do it properly, tell them a lie . . . OK, come when you can. You've got the address . . . yes, it will be nice. 'Bye . . .

35 James's flat, night

Susan sits cross-legged in the centre of James's bea. James lies along one edge, head propped on elbows. They've been drinking coffee. We have the sense of a long evening of intimate talk, but not much else so far. A pause before Susan speaks.

JAMES Why not stay?

SUSAN I have to be up early. (*She stands.*)

JAMES Me too.

SUSAN (*straightening herself at the mirror. James standing close*). Two or three years ago I would have stayed. And fucked you.

JAMES Too late. Just my luck.

He stands behind her and kisses her neck. She turns and they kiss. Susan pulls away. She taps James's nose with her forefinger.

SUSAN Now I'm more wary. I must be getting old.

She reaches for her coat. James helps her.

JAMES You don't trust me.

SUSAN I don't trust anyone. That's what comes of working in television.

JAMES In radio we're different.

SUSAN I bet. Thanks for the drink.

He opens the door.

JAMES I might see you in Norfolk over the weekend.

SUSAN (*smiling*). You just might.

She closes the door on her smile.

36 Squash court, day

A day later. A glass-fronted squash court. James and Jeremy are into a game. Both are inept and very unfit. We come in

*on a rally. Jeremy misses an easy ball and lets his racket drop.
James sits down with his back to the wall. Jeremy gets his
cigarettes from a corner of the court. They inhale smoke as if
it were fresh air.*

JEREMY That's enough of that.

JAMES We've been playing ten minutes for Christ's sake.

JEREMY Far too long.

*A pause. Some keen squash players appear at the door, peer
in and go away.*

JAMES What have you been up to?

JEREMY Well, everyone's desperate for a new Falklands angle.
Purdy's come up with a real dog. Workers' rights in
Argentina. So I've been running round getting people to do
things. But no one's keen. Workers' rights. When did anyone
on that paper give a damn about workers' rights? I said to
Purdy, 'Look, tits, bingo, jingo, horoscope, sport, celebs,
gossip and the occasional firm stand on—'

JAMES The torture of small children—

JEREMY On the torture of *very* small children, but don't start
telling them about their rights—

JAMES Hold those rights.

JEREMY Tame those rights . . . you know, we're even
freighting in a couple of exiled Argie trade unionists from Paris
for a TV tie-in. One of them had his balls tap-danced on by
the secret police. The other one had to be hosed off the wall
of his cell after the police – yes, my good man?

*A muscular coach in a tracksuit, is rapping on the glass door.
And opening it. He wears a short towel around his neck.*

I'm sorry. This is a private conversation. You'll have to wait.
Outside.

COACH You can't smoke in here. This is a squash court.

JEREMY Well we booked it for a smoke, didn't we, James?

JAMES And we're not quite finished.

COACH Come on. Out!

A few players have gathered to watch outside.

JEREMY The court is ours for another half hour. Please run
along.

*The coach advances into the court, picks up their rackets and
stands over them. He pushes a racket under Jeremy's chin.*

COACH I said, out.

JAMES On the other hand, we might be more comfortable at
the bar. I've got some news on Suez.

JEREMY (*racket still under his chin*) A serious drink might be
of use, I suppose.

37 James's flat, morning

*James adjusts his tie in the mirror. The phone rings. Lay over
James's voice into Scenes 38 and 39.*

JAMES Oh, hello, Dad, I've been meaning to phone you. How
is she? . . . Oh . . . in the night? . . . Oh God. What does
the doctor say? . . . Look, I will, I will. I promise. But it's
impossible at the moment, now with the crisis on. I'm

working night and day . . . Look, tell her I'll come as soon
as I can. I promise . . . Look, Dad, I've got to dash. Give
her my love. Yes . . . bye.

38 Brixton, Day

*James walks down a Brixton street, down a narrow road to a
set of lock-up garages. A group of black kids are playing
football here. James steps round puddles, careful not to muddy
his shoes. He scowls at the kids and unlocks his garage.*

*James backs his car out of the garage. An early sixties Jaguar
saloon. He gets out to close the garage door. The game of
football rages around his car, as if it was not there.*

39 Car-wash, day

*Ten minutes later. A car-wash. From the driver's point of view
we watch the revolving brushes advance and engulf the car.*

*The phone conversation ends. James reaches down and pushes
a tape into the car tape deck. We will hear the recording all
through James's journey, to Scene 41.*

LECTURER (*voice-over*) You see, if we talk of a nation, like an
individual, acting emotionally, we can also speak of it acting
deceitfully. Britain and France had entered into a secret
agreement with the Arabs' deadly enemy, the Israelis. The
agreement was signed or initialled by the Foreign Secretary,

Selwyn Lloyd on or about 23 October, at Sevres. The Israelis were to attack Egypt on an agreed date. British planes based in Cyprus were to precision bomb Egyptian airfields to protect Israeli cities from retaliation. After putting out an ultimatum to both sides to withdraw to ten miles from the Canal, which of course the Egyptians would have to ignore since the Canal is a hundred miles inside their territory, the British and the French would invade on the pretext of 'separating the combatants'. That became something of a catch phrase – 'separating the combatants'.

40 City, day

James's car makes its way through the City.

41 M11, day

An hour later. The M11. James's car speeds away from us.

42 North Norfolk, day

An hour and a half later. James drives along a country road.

43 The Barrington House, day

A small boy, Tom, peers over a wall at James's car as it sweeps into the drive.

44 Library, day

Five minutes later. The Barrington house. The library. James waits alone. The house stands in its own grounds – an old rectory, spacious, but not over-grand. Much charm. Nineteenth- and twentieth-century oil paintings, a serious reader's library. Pleasant disorder, but no squalor. There is one housekeeper.

Somewhere in the house a phone rings. There are footsteps. James crosses to a window which faces out over the garden which is large and well-kept. At some distance away a gardener is raking leaves. Another man comes and talks to him, and then disappears from sight. This is Matthew, Ann Barrington's husband.

The door opens slowly. Tom, the ten-year-old son of Matthew, stares at James.

After a pause.

JAMES Hullo.

TOM Hullo.

JAMES I'm waiting for your mother.

TOM She said awfully sorry, make yourself comfortable, she won't be long.

JAMES Thanks.

TOM Why not sit down and wait?

JAMES OK, I will.

TOM She's not my mother, anyway. My mother's in Italy.

JAMES Oh, I see.

TOM Have you come to talk about me?

JAMES Not at all. History.

At this Tom leaves the door and advances into the room.

TOM What period?

JAMES Suez. 1956.

TOM Do you want to hear my list of English Kings and Queens?

JAMES All right.

TOM It goes from Henry VIII.
(*In rapid monotone.*)

Henry VIII, Edward VI, Mary,
Elizabeth I, James I, Charles I,
Charles II, James II, William and
Mary, Ann, George I, II, II and IV,
Victoria, Edward VII, George V,
Edward VIII, George VI,
Elizabeth II.

JAMES What about the Cromwells?

TOM They don't count.

Ann Barrington comes in. Aged about fifty-five, very attractive still, and fit.

ANN Mr Penfield. I am sorry to have kept you.

JAMES It's kind of you to see me.

ANN Tom, Daddy would like to see you in the garden. And will you ask Betty to bring us some coffee. And remember to say please.

Tom leaves. They watch as he closes the door with exaggerated care.

ANN He's a little unhappy. I hope he wasn't a nuisance.

JAMES He was delightful.

45 Study, day

Ten minutes later. Ann sits behind her desk. James sits across from her. The housekeeper sets down a tray and leaves.

Ann appraises James and deals with the coffee, and for the first time in the film we take a long, hard look at him too. The light flatters. The notebook at his side, his patience and deference, the well-cut suit . . . he is at least credible.

ANN My first husband worked for the BBC. I doubt if anyone there remembers him now, just another long dead, diligent administrator. He would have been useful to them now, you know. He was involved in the fight to preserve the BBC's independence during the Suez crisis – one of the few things he was passionate about. I became involved too. I started work on a book that would have been published on the tenth anniversary of Suez. Then he died, and I lost the will to write it. By the time I was over his death, other books had been published, and it wasn't worth going on.

JAMES What a shame.

ANN It wasn't much more than a pot boiler. Suez was very important for our generation. I didn't want it to be forgotten. And that's why I'd like to be able to help you. But really Mr Penfield, I looked through my notes before you came, they're all very much out of date, there's been so much published since. I don't think I'm your man.

JAMES (*smiling, uncertain*) Well, I am a great admirer of your work. I read your books on Chartism when I was still at school. I'm a journalist, not a historian. There are questions of method, and approach. I wondered . . .

ANN I see. Are you a socialist, Mr Penfield?

JAMES Yes.

ANN Good. Suez was a minefield for both Parties.

46 Garden, day

The garden, same time. Tom wanders aimlessly near the house. He comes to one of the library windows and peers in.

Unobserved, he watches Ann and James. Ann is speaking. James interrupts, Ann nods, James writes something down in his notebook.

Tom hears his father in the distance calling his name. He leaves the window and runs.

47 Conservatory, day

Lunchtime. A table spread with white tablecloth, salads and wine. Set for two.

ANN My husband apologizes for not joining us. He's taking Tom into town. It's not too cold for you, Mr Penfield?

JAMES It's fine, thank you.

ANN Since you are a friend of my daughter's, I think I'm entitled to call you James, don't you think?
JAMES Please do. I was beginning to wonder who this Mr Penfield was.

ANN And I'd like you to call me Ann.

James raises his glass.

JAMES To Ann.

ANN To James. I remember what it was I was going to say. We were talking about forgetfulness. The Czech writer Kundera has one of his characters say that the struggle of man against tyranny is the struggle of memory against forgetting.

JAMES History books are first onto the bonfires.

ANN No. If we leave the remembering to historians then the struggle is already lost. Everyone must have a memory, everyone needs to be a historian. In this country, for example, we're in danger of losing hard-won freedoms by dozing off in a perpetual present.

James is uneasy, a little out of his depth.

Here I am lecturing you. Have some pâté.

JAMES Thanks.

A pause. Ann has already emptied her glass. James has hardly touched his. Ann refills her own. Then James, lightly, wanting to be back on familiar ground.

So I can go ahead and be a historian without feeling like a poseur. I shall be fulfilling a citizen's duty.

ANN If you like. But don't be too modest, James. The citizen's duty is to remember, not necessarily to write books. You are highly qualified. You're a responsible journalist doing what sounds to me like a very demanding job. Every day you take decisions that depend on your sense of history. A genuine tyranny would have to get rid of people like you.

JAMES You're kind to be so encouraging.

ANN I think you'll do very well.

She smiles and briefly touches James's hand. James looks up, impassive.

48 Back gate to garden, day

Ann and James are returning from an after-lunch walk. We have a glimpse of the landscape we will see more of on James's return.

As they talk they arrive through a back gate into the Barrington garden. A jet fighter races through the sky.

ANN I've met some of her colleagues. I'm afraid they struck me as rather empty people. Very ambitious, and charming too. But not serious. No politics.

They walk on.

I do worry about Susan. Have you known her long? She hasn't mentioned you.

JAMES Actually, we've only just met. But we're quite good friends.

ANN It's a pity she couldn't make it up here today.

JAMES Yes.

ANN She'll be here next weekend. Why don't you come too, James? I'll show you the marshes properly. If you're lucky you might even see the first of the geese arriving from Siberia.

JAMES Well, I'd hate to be a nuisance.

ANN Don't be silly. I'll look out some more Suez material for you. You'll be very welcome.

49 Front of house, day

They come round the front of the house to James's car. He opens the door and shakes Ann's hand.

JAMES Thank you.

ANN We'll see you next week, and if . . .

Matthew's car comes sweeping up the drive. Tom is in the front seat. Matthew stops his car so that his front door is by James's.

Matthew is fifty. A director of commercials for cinema and television. Breezy, chunky-faced, keen to be taken seriously. Essentially good-humoured.

ANN I wish you wouldn't drive so fast, Mat, dearest.

MATTHEW I'll get a bike. I promise. Hi! Just off?

Matthew and James shake hands over the car doors.

ANN Matthew, my husband. James. James is coming to stay next weekend.

MATTHEW Very good. Well, I'll see you then.

He strides away with Tom.

Come on, Tom. Let's see if we can get this thing working.

James pulls away. Ann stands watching him till he is out of sight, and a little longer after that.

50 A149, day

Ten minutes later. James drives along the A149 near Clay. He has the window wide open, the radio on. The great expanse of salt marsh is to his right. The huge sky. The mood is triumphant.

51 Central Norfolk, day

Half an hour later. A lonely road in central Norfolk. James brings the car to a sudden halt. He switches off the engine. In the silence we are able to hear the car cassette player.

As it plays, James walks round the car till he finds his flat tyre.

He rummages with growing ill-temper in the boot. Two cases of empty wine bottles, a mildewed towel and swimming trunks, but no jack.

LECTURER (*voice over*) There was a real desire on the British part to appear virtuous while behaving aggressively, and the pursuit of virtue led to many lies being told, most notable the Prime Minister's in the House of Commons on 20 December when he said that there was 'no foreknowledge that Israel would attack Egypt'. Perhaps we should reverse the question and ask ourselves to what extent individuals behave like governments, who are bound to act in the national interest which in turn is rarely separable from the government's interest, or that of the class it represents . . .

Furious, he goes to the front of the car and snaps off the tape machine, and stands jiggling his keys in the vast silence.

A minute later. James sets off. The immensity of the landscape, the incongruousness of his clothes . . .

52 Lonely road, day

James, walking.

53 Road through wood, day

The road passes through a wood. When Betty speaks, it surprises both James and us.

BETTY Are you the man from the BBC?

She stands at the head of a little grass track that leads into a wood. She carries a plastic carrier bag. She is almost childlike in her friendliness.

JAMES What?

BETTY Sorry. I didn't mean to frighten you. I thought you must be from the BBC. (*She advances.*) We've been waiting, see. And you don't exactly look like a farmer. I'm Betty.

They shake hands.

JAMES James Penfield.

BETTY Come and meet the others. They've been waiting for you.

54 Woods, airfield perimeter, day

James follows Betty through the woods. A rumbling and whining noise increases in violence and becomes deafening once they leave the wood and cross open ground towards a Military Air Base. The Peace Camp is near the perimeter fence.

A ramshackle collection of tents, caravans, a tepee and a rough wooden shelter which is the communal area. A fire burns here. Various peace signs, Women's Movement sign and slogan. ('Fight War, Not Wars' etc.)

Three women are sitting around the fire. A little further off a man is chopping wood. One of the women, Carmen, is over sixty. The other two are in their thirties. The man, Pete, is a vintage hippy. A good mix of regional accents among the campers.

Betty leads James to the fire.

BETTY I found *a* man from the BBC, but he's not *the* man.

CARMEN Never mind. We'll just have to make do. Would you like a cup of tea? Jill, give the young man your cup.

JAMES (*dodging smoke from the fire*) Thank you.

CARMEN Sit on that log, dear.

JILL Be careful though, it wobbles.

The others laugh.

JAMES Er, listen, I . . . I've got a puncture. I wondered if I might borrow a jack.

JILL *and* CAROL Pete!

JAMES Sorry to be a nuisance.

Pete ambles over. Inscrutable behind much hair. He registers no awareness of James. He smokes a roll-up.

CARMEN Pete, do we have a jack?

Pete inhales, considers and nods almost imperceptibly.

Could you look it out for our friend?

Pete nods again and returns to chopping wood.

JILL Is the tea all right? I didn't ask you if you wanted sugar.

JAMES It's fine, thanks.

CARMEN Now first of all, tell us your name

JAMES Penfield. James Penfield.

CARMEN This is Jill, Carol, Betty, Mandy, Louise, Pete over there, and I'm Carmen.

The women smile and murmur hello as they are introduced. Their friendliness progressively disorientates James.

There's another fifteen of us out at a meeting.

CAROL Would you like us to show you round the camp.

CARMEN Let him drink his tea, poor man. I don't know what's happened to this other fellow. He said he'd be here at three.

JILL Lost!

BETTY What do you do at the BBC, James?

JAMES I work in radio news, in London.

A chorus of 'Oh well then . . .' and 'Great!'

JAMES But I'm not an interviewer or a correspondent.

CARMEN That doesn't matter. As long as we can get our message through to someone there. Jill, where are those handouts?

JILL They're back here somewhere. They're a bit crumpled.

Pete hands a jack to James.

JAMES Oh, great. Thanks.

Now James has his jack he begins to back away.

CARMEN Give them here. This tells you how the Women's Peace Camp came to be set up. All local women at first, then we had support from women and men all over the country.

JAMES Very good.

JILL The response has been just amazing.

JAMES Yes.

CARMEN And this sheet tells you all about the base, the number of missiles they're going to have, what they think they're for and so on.

CAROL We've had the local radio down here.

JAMES Terrific.

CARMEN But what we need is national coverage. It's difficult with this Falklands madness going on. Do you think you might be able to do something when you get back?

JAMES I'll suggest it. Remember though, we're news, not features. It might help if you could get yourselves attacked by the police. Anyway, I'll be back with this soon. Thanks.

BETTY (*close up, eyes wide*) Ordinary people everywhere are saying 'No, we don't want these terrible weapons!' *That's* news!

JAMES I won't be a moment.

55 Peace Camp, evening

James drives down the road towards the airbase. He stops his car well short of the camp. He takes the jack from the car and walks towards the camp. There are more people now moving in and out of the light of the fire. The sounds of voices, laughter, mostly female. A meal is being cooked.

James sets down the jack where it can be found. He has been observed throughout by Pete, from the shadows. He speaks as James is turning back towards his car.

PETE Off then?

JAMES Er, yes, I put the jack by the . . . hut there. Thanks for your help . . . I . . . I have to be getting back . . . so . . . see you. And thanks . . . and . . . all the best.

Pete watches James walk away.

56 Television company entrance/stairs, afternoon

London. A day later. The television company where Susan works. James is late. The lift is out of order. He runs up several flights of stairs with diminishing energy.

57 Screening room, afternoon

Breathless, James bursts into the screening room. Susan is seated. Jeremy stands near her, leaning against a desk, smoking. By contrast, they are calm.

JEREMY Fortunate that I was here to keep Susan entertained.

JAMES Sorry. Got held up. What are you doing here?

JEREMY Delivering gossip and goodwill. It seems we'll both be doing Brighton.

He starts to put on his coat.

Perhaps you should come too.

JAMES (*to Susan*) Will it be fun?

SUSAN It was last year.

JEREMY We might be able to dig out a couple of Suez survivors for you.

JAMES Perhaps I will, then.

JEREMY (*kissing on the cheek first Susan, then James*) I'm off. Let's meet. You promised to tell me about Norfolk.

JAMES I'll ring you.

A brief pause and a slight awkwardness after Jeremy leaves.

SUSAN (*into microphone*) I think we're ready now, thank you. And how was Norfolk? Did you get on with my mother?

JAMES I think she liked me.

SUSAN Did she talk about me?

JAMES No. We talked about history, and Siberian Geese.

The lights go down.

We see a series of film clips about Suez: crowd scenes in Cairo; footage of the Fleet on its way from Malta; the actual invasion; parachutes; Eden at Downing Street; Lloyd at the airport; the protest meeting at Trafalgar Square; fighting in Suez streets.

James sneaks occasional looks at Susan throughout. We see her in profile, lit by the screen.

SUSAN (*as the first pictures come up*) It's not in chronological order. There's an hour of stuff, of which the director has to choose four minutes. What'll happen is that I'll choose it for him . . . Does he look like a man on speed?

Our two minute sequence is presented to represent an hour of film. When at last it is over and the lights come up, there is a moment of stupefaction. Susan yawns and prepares to leave.

SUSAN Do you think she's invited you up for her sake or for mine?

JAMES (*kissing Susan's fingers*) I haven't really thought about it.

SUSAN (*smiling, mischievous*) Well, you should.

James kisses Susan. She complies rather than responds.

*Susan disengages herself gently and gathers her things.
She stands.*

Well, must get on.

58 Newsroom, early morning

A day or two later. People are drifting out to go down the corridor to the morning news conference. James is one of the last to leave. On his way out he meets Charles, the newsreader from Scene Two.

JAMES Charles! I didn't know you were back. Have a good holiday?

CHARLES Not too bad, thanks. How have you been?

JAMES Working hard on that book I was telling you about. Coming to the meeting?

CHARLES I'm not sure I can face it.

JAMES Keep me company.

59 Corridor, early morning

James steers Charles out of the newsroom and along the corridor. Only slowly does it become apparent that Charles is in a state of distress.

JAMES How's Mary?

CHARLES She's fine. Well, actually we've broken up. It's all over.

JAMES No. That's terrible, Charles. What happened?

CHARLES (*on the edge of tears*) Look, I'd rather you didn't ask me questions. I can't talk about it.

They have reached the News Conference Room, but Charles walks on down the corridor to nurse his grief out of sight.

60 News conference room, morning

The news conference room. Ten minutes later. The same Editor. The same matter-of-factness and slight boredom.

EDITOR . . . as it happens they got all their facts wrong anyway. I checked up. We reported the big peace march on Hyde Park last October, and a march on NATO headquarters in the spring, *and* the death of whatsisname last month, the old CND man . . .

He looks round. It is not clear that anyone is listening.

What really gets to them, though they'll never admit it, these types, is that we give both sides, theirs *and* the government's. Multilateralists and unilateralists. Hawks *and* doves. As far as they're concerned, there's only one side to the question. Nuclear weapons are bad. Full stop. End of discussion. Anyone who says there's more to it than that is . . . what was it . . .

(He picks up a newspaper cutting.)

'under cover of an authoritative news service, propagating a military definition of reality.'

He pauses, relaxes into professional indifference.

Still. With the party conferences coming up in the autumn there's bound to be some action on that front and we'd be doing something anyway. It won't *all* be Falklands business. James, is there something in there for us, if we could tie it in with something else?

JAMES Well, it's all a bit cranky and small scale. Vegetarians, hippies, disturbed housewives. Local radio story, I'd say, if that. They're mad.

EDITOR Oh well. Just an idea. Now. Can we talk about this radio-car cock-up yesterday. Chris?

61 Newsroom studio, late morning

Two hours later. The studio. James and Charles sit at the table, as in Scene Three. Charles reads. He is obviously distressed but his voice remains under control. James watches anxiously.

CHARLES It was an emotional occasion. Hundreds of small craft led by six fire tugs making fountains of water formed an escort flotilla, and four Wasp helicopters flew past in salute. In the City the Financial Times Ordinary Shares Index was down ten points an hour ago at 529.8. BBC Radio News.

In the Control Room, the minute hand of the clock reaches five past the hour; the sweep hand reaches the twelve on Charles's last word. The Controller pushes a button. Charles slumps forward.

JAMES My God that was close! Well done, Charles. I knew you wouldn't let me down. But God! We almost didn't make it.

James is standing, gathering papers. He bustles out, indifferent. We close in on Charles. Unseen by anyone, he is just beginning to cry.

62 James's flat, evening

James is typing rapidly. There is a growing pile of typewritten sheets to one side. We go over his shoulder and look closely at the map, Egypt, the desert . . .

63 The Barrington house, Norfolk, late morning

A few days later. James has just arrived and switched his engine off. But for the wind and birdsong, silence.

There is no reply when he tries the front door. A note pinned to the door reads: 'Gone for a walk. Follow footpath. Susan.'

64 Dyke, day

James walks along the dyke, across the marshes. Below him, on the sand, in the distance, are two figures. James stops to watch them. Matthew and Susan are deep in conversation – evidently a serious matter. They seem to be making an agreement. Matthew puts his head on Susan's shoulder, and they walk on, unaware of James.

65 Dining-room, night

A burst of laughter. It is dinner. Seated are Ann, Matthew, Tom, Susan, James and Jacek, a professor from Central Europe, mid-sixties, an old friend of Ann's. Betty, the housemaid, serves.

JACEK (*heavy accent*) The second is less pleasant. A Pole is confronted by a German and a Russian soldier. Which should he shoot first? The German first, the Russian second. Duty before pleasure.

A more subdued response.

TOM I've heard that one at school.

JACEK Then you are a well-educated young man. (*To Ann.*) Tom has been reciting his English kings and queens to me.

JAMES And to me.

JACEK Haven't you socialist historians in the West made kings and queens out of date in schools?

ANN We keep trying.

MATTHEW I can tell you that the history of the monarchy is alive and well in the national memory. I shot a commercial – a series of vignettes of kings and queens – Henry VIII, Mary—

TOM Elizabeth I.

MATTHEW Elizabeth I, and so on – and we had a fantastic response.

SUSAN What were you advertising?

MATTHEW Oh, some new lager.

JACEK I'm pleased to hear that there is at least some national memory. I agree with Ann that the British forget too quickly. Here you have enviable freedoms, and yet no monuments to those who struggled to win them for you. Now that is why I think there is hope for the Poles, whoever occupies their country. They remember their dates, and they keep adding to them. December 1981, Gdansk 1980, 1976, 1970. Katyn 1940, 1922 and so on. It's a subversive list. Say it out loud on the streets of Warsaw and you might get arrested.

During this last speech of Jacek's we see James trying to catch Susan's eye. She glances up and looks away.

66 Stairs, night

An hour later.

Wine glass in hand James goes upstairs. He comes to Tom's room.

67 Tom's room, night

Susan has been seeing Tom into bed.

James watches from the doorway. She kisses her brother and turns out the light.

TOM Don't close the door. Don't turn out the hall light.

SUSAN I won't. Goodnight.

TOM 'Night.

James and Susan linger in the semi-darkness outside Tom's room. From downstairs comes the sound of boisterous conversation.

JAMES I haven't seen much of you.

SUSAN No. It's a bit of a madhouse. For some reason a lot of my mother's friends specialize in monologues.

JAMES He's all right, the professor.

Tom comes out of his room.

TOM Ah, Susy, it . . .

SUSAN Tom . . . bed! Go on.

Tom retreats into his bedroom. James and Susan move to the head of the stairs.

JAMES Look, will you come on a walk with me tomorrow?

SUSAN I might.

JAMES Might?

ANN (*calling from below*) Susan, James, are you up there?

SUSAN Hello, Mummy.

Ann comes half-way up the stairs.

ANN Betty's made some coffee. Do you want some?

SUSAN Yes, we do.

ANN Well, we're in the library.

Ann lingers a moment. She wants James downstairs. As soon as she has gone, he kisses Susan.

JAMES Might?

SUSAN (*strokes his face*) Yes. Might. Remember, you're here to talk to my mother.

She leads the way downstairs.

68 Library, night

The library. A fire burns. Ann pours the coffee and is highly aware of James when he comes in. Jacek is a little drunk.

JACEK Ah, Susan, James. Come and judge. I am interrogating Matthew. I am asking him how a director of advertisements and a socialist get along so well together. How does the lion lie down with the lamb.

ANN By staying in town all week. And lying down with several lambs.

MATTHEW Not so. We meet half way. Ann has grown very fond of her material comforts. She even owns land with keep out signs posted on the boundaries. And I . . .

ANN (*wearily, to James*) I bought a wood because a local farmer was going to cut it down. The signs were already there.

JACEK And you . . .

MATTHEW I earn so much money at what I do that I can't even begin to defend it. I used to shoot a whole line about the value and necessity of advertising . . .

ANN You were more interesting then.

MATTHEW . . . but now I'm an agnostic. So is Ann, if she'd only admit it.

ANN Come on, James. Defend me from this tripe.

Expectant pause. Susan smirks. James is out of his depth.

JAMES Well, there's no reason why a socialist shouldn't like comfort, or own a wood, or be very rich. The problem is making all that available to everybody . . .

All except Ann groan dismissively.

MATTHEW Rubbish!

JACEK Ah, if everybody is to have everything, then you need to plan very carefully, you need to control the future. This is the tragedy of Marxism. The future is not ours to control, nothing turns out as we plan it. (*To Ann.*) You remember that charming note of Enzensberger's, quoting Hobsbawm? A congress of Spanish anarchists in 1898 looked forward to a glorious future after the revolution – a world of incredibly tall shining buildings, with elevators that would save climbing stairs, electric light for all, garbage disposal chutes and wonderful household gadgets. This vision is now a reality in our cities, the victory has been won and it looks just like defeat . . .

Susan yawns conspicuously. Everybody turns.

SUSAN (*unrepentant*) Sorry. Tired.

69 Kitchen, morning

The following morning. If possible, a beautiful day. Betty is washing up a large pile of breakfast things. From outside, the sound of much hilarity.

70 Garden, morning

On the back lawn Tom, Susan and Matthew are playing football. To one side, Jacek leans on his stick and watches.

71 Library, morning

*The library. Ann and James sit facing each other by the
fireplace. The game of football can be heard. From where
James sits he can see past and into the gardens, the occasional
glimpse of Susan, the enticing sunlight.*

ANN The references are to Hansard or to newspapers. I
haven't got the actual speeches now. You'll have to chase
them up.

JAMES I will, thanks.

ANN These are transcripts of various radio broadcasts,
including Gaitskill's, the one they tried to stop. You ought
to have that . . .

Betty knocks and enters.

BETTY Excuse me. Phone call for Mr Penfield.

ANN Take it here.

JAMES Thanks. Hello . . . how did you get this number? I see.
Look, I'm really sorry about last week, I . . . no, I'm up
here researching something I . . . is she? . . . well, don't they
have painkillers for that? . . . Oh, yeah . . . Look, tell her
I'll be there . . . I can't just drop everything. It'll probably be
the day after tomorrow . . . Right . . . OK . . . yes, goodbye.
(*To Ann.*) It's a relative of mine. She's not very well. (*He sits
down again.*) I'm sorry. What were you saying?

72 Garden, day

A couple of hours later. Susan sits on a bench re-tying the lace of her walking boot. James stands, waiting.

SUSAN Jeremy phoned this morning.

JAMES What did he want?

SUSAN He's making plans for Brighton. He thought we could travel down together.

JAMES That'll be fun.

SUSAN In your car.

JAMES Why not.

Ann appears from the house. Tom follows.

ANN Hello. Anyone for a walk? Tom isn't, I can tell you.

JAMES Well, we were just . . .

SUSAN Don't you want to walk, Tom?

TOM No.

SUSAN Actually, I've been once today already. I'll stay here with him.

ANN James and I have been indoors all morning.

SUSAN Well, he's very keen to go.

She walks with Tom towards the house.

JAMES Susan . . .

Holding Tom's hand, she turns and smiles.

SUSAN See you when you get back.

James has been quickly outmanoeuvred by Susan. He stands awkwardly for a moment, collecting himself.

ANN Shall we go?

JAMES Yes.

73 Dyke, day

The dyke across the marshes, the sand dunes, the sea. During Ann's monologue (broken up where appropriate) we see the two sometimes in close, sometimes as minute figures in this immense landscape.

James follows Ann along the dyke.

They stop and she points out a wooded hill, well inland.

Later . . .

ANN Then I began to listen to what the well-off were saying about the poor now – the war had just ended, and the language was much the same as it had been before the first Reform Act.
A small minority thought that England was really theirs, they had made it, they owned it. The rest, the wage earners, were foreigners, outsiders intent on wrecking it all.

JAMES Didn't Evelyn Waugh say that the country under Atlee seemed to be under enemy occupation?

ANN Did he? I left school and worked for the Labour Party. My older brother, George, had just been killed in Greece, and he'd been an active member. I hero-worshipped him. He was twenty-five years old . . . (*She trails off.*) It was an exciting time for us, those first couple of years after the war. We thought the country was about to become a true democracy. I can understand why people of your generation want to write about that time. They feel betrayed. They want to know what went wrong.

JAMES What went wrong?

ANN Oh, many things. Inertia . . . Stalin and the Cold War . . . a failure of nerve. We took the seediest, most inefficient fifth of the economy into State care, paid out millions for it, put the same old duffers in charge. A new broom with very old bristles. When the Tories were returned, I went and sat in the BM and wrote my little book on Chartism.

Later. Walking home.

I don't like admitting it, but the truth is, I am happy. Matthew's right. I like comfort. I like doing my own work and not having to teach. I love my house and the garden, and my wood. (*She stops.*) And I'm very happy walking here with you. (*She takes his hand.*) You have such a quiet, strong sense of purpose. Energy. I think I'll rely on you to take the uncomfortable stands in life. I've done my bit.

They smile at each other.

Ann moves in to kiss James passionately. He complies.

A jet fighter flies in low over the marshes.

74 Drawing-room, evening

Susan and Tom, who wears pyjamas and dressing-gown, are playing chess. James watches Susan. Tom is noisily, bossily instructing her in the rules. Matthew is approaching James, about to speak.

MATTHEW I just might give you a ring when we get back to London. There's one or two things I'd like to . . . Will you let me have your number before you leave? Have you ever watched a commercial being made?

JAMES No.

MATTHEW Well, it's worth seeing.

Ann appears in the doorway.

ANN James . . .

There is a moment of awkwardness. James squeezes past Matthew and goes towards Ann.

JAMES Excuse me.

75 Library, evening

The library. A moment later. James has just come in.
Ann hands him a silver framed photograph.

ANN I wanted to show you. It was taken six months before he died.

The resemblance between James and the dead brother should

*be clear. James studies the photograph. He looks up. Ann is
gazing at him steadily.*

76 Dining-room, night

*Half an hour later. Ann, Matthew, Susan and James. A certain
strain. The sound of knives and forks only.*

In the hall the phone rings. They hear Betty pick it up.

Still holding the receiver she pushes open the dining-room door.

BETTY (*to Matthew*) It's for you, Mr Fox.

*The others go on eating, acutely aware of Matthew's
conversation.*

MATTHEW (*from the hall*). Hello . . . Oh, hi . . . well, you
know . . .

He pushes the door shut with his foot.

James looks at Susan.

Susan glances at her mother.

*Ann knows it is one of Matthew's girlfriends. She goes on
eating, a brave but failing attempt to appear untouched.*

77 James's bedroom, night

Very late, the same night.

From the point of view of an intruder we move into the room. James is asleep.

ANN'S VOICE (*whispers*) James . . . James.

He snaps awake. We see what he sees. Ann sits on the edge of his bed, in tears.

She touches his face.

She leans over and embraces him.

78 James's bedroom, night

A little later. The beside lamp is on. James lies still, his expression numb. The bedclothes are in disarray. His bedroom door is just closing.

79 Newsroom, late morning

The Newsroom at its busiest, as in Scene One. Linger on the activity before finding James. He sits writing a report in longhand, referring to News Agency material. Much dictating going on around him, so that Philip who sits across from him has almost to shout to be heard. He has picked up a phone and is covering the mouthpiece.

PHILIP It's that lady from Norfolk again.

JAMES I'm not here.

PHILIP I'm terribly sorry. He doesn't seem to be here . . . No . . . Yes, if I see him, I will . . . Goodbye. She's going to phone back.

JAMES Next time tell her I've gone away.

CHARLES Aha. James giving some woman the old heave-ho.

JAMES (*grim smile*) Exactly that.

80 James's flat, evening

Tight shot of Edward on the phone.

EDWARD Hello, you don't know me. My name's Edward Long. I'm a friend of James Penfield. He asked me to phone you. I don't know what any of this means, but he said you would understand . . . Yes, that's right. He said he's got to go away for a while, and that he'll be writing to you and please don't try and contact him . . . Hello?

Pulling away, we see where we are. James sits in a chair reading a magazine.

God, that was terrible. Don't ever ask me another favour like that.

JAMES You were wonderful. I'm very grateful.

EDWARD She hung up. Why couldn't you just write to her?

JAMES I will, sooner or later. (*Standing.*) Trouble is I hate writing letters. Now, where are we going to eat?

81 Film studio, morning

What we see first is the actual set and only subsequently the surrounding technical apparatus of film-making.

We are suddenly in a deeply contented pre-war middle-class sitting-room. Guide track: sweet, period music. Dad sits in an armchair reading a newspaper. A pipe is near at hand. To one side, a wireless. At his feet, a girl plays with a doll; a boy plays with a model steam engine.

Mum enters with a tray of steaming hot drinks. As she sets down the tray on the arm of Dad's chair, the music peaks and the children half rise and arrange themselves on either side of Dad's legs. Everyone smiles up at Mum.

Once this has unfolded, we pull back to see the camera crew, continuity, make-up etc. James is standing to one side watching.

MATTHEW And . . . cut. Steve?

STEVE (*camera-man*) Not the best, guv'nor.

MATTHEW Right . . . we'll go again, please.

Matthew to ad lib instructions to actors and crew. He notices James.

James, good, you made it. We're just going to do one more take, then we'll break for lunch.

The commercial is set up and shot again, with Matthew continuing to give ad libbed directions. As soon as the take is over, Matthew snatches his jacket, gives a quick kiss to a young woman who could well be his current lover, and steers James out of the studio.

Right, James. Come on. Let's go before the clients get hold of me.

82 Pub, day

Lunchtime. Matthew stands at the bar where he is buying drinks and lunch. Then the two men sit at a small table face to face.

MATTHEW I'll tell you another thing. We might have led the world once into the Industrial Revolution, now we lead with television commercials. We're the best, it's as simple as that. Even the Americans will admit it now . . . the camera work, the acting, the scripts, special effects. We've got the lot. Nearly all the good directors here have ambitions to make serious films. (*A sudden laugh.*) That food you're eating.

JAMES Yes.

MATTHEW What would you call it?

JAMES I dunno. Ploughman's Lunch.

MATTHEW Ploughman's Lunch. Traditional English fare.

JAMES U-huh.

MATTHEW In fact it's the invention of an advertising campaign they ran in the early sixties to encourage people to eat in pubs. A completely successful fabrication of the past, the Ploughman's Lunch was.

We look at James's plate, the unappetizing food. Matthew takes a long drink

Listen, James. There's something else I want to talk to you about.

Matthew pauses.

I'm pretty broadminded, and I'd rather be frank than have everybody misunderstanding one another. If you see what I mean.

James does not.

Susan told me that your visits to Norfolk had . . . well, an ulterior motive.

JAMES She said that?

MATTHEW You weren't really interested in Suez at all. Incredibly enough, you were interested in my wife.

JAMES Now listen . . .

MATTHEW No, no, let me go on before you get the wrong idea. Ann and I have kept to our separate bedrooms for the last three years. And I can't imagine that Susan hasn't hinted at the kind of life I lead in London. I'm not telling you how to run your affairs. I'm just saying . . . I don't mind. I'm giving you permission.

We are close in on James's reaction.

83 James's car, early morning

James drives towards Susan's flat. Jeremy sprawls in the back seat, slowly peeling the foil from a champagne bottle. Both are well-dressed. As they draw up outside Susan's flat, Jeremy leans forward and murmurs in James's ear.

JEREMY Still in love?

JAMES I'm not sure.

He presses the horn and gets out. Jeremy gets out too. Susan comes down the steps. She is also smartly dressed. She kisses James. He takes her small suitcase and puts it in the boot. She kisses Jeremy.

JEREMY Darling Susan. You look like an angel. But where's your hat?

SUSAN Oh no!

JEREMY They won't let you in without one.

James hands Susan into the front seat.

JEREMY Brighton, James!

84 London street, day

The car slips through the London traffic.

85 James's car, day

In the car, a few minutes later. Much hilarity. Susan is holding a glass ready as Jeremy eases out the cork.

SUSAN Don't point it at James!

JEREMY Voilà!

The cork flies. The champagne is poured. Susan hands a glass to James.

To the ninety-ninth conference of the National Union of Conservative and Unionist Associations!

All repeat the toast with various stumbling inaccuracies.

86 Car park, Brighton, day

James drives into a multi-storey car park. Jeremy gets out of the car and goes to look at the view which is of modern office developments.

JEREMY Ahh – the seaside! Isn't it heavenly!

Susan joins Jeremy.

SUSAN Gorgeous.

Jeremy is taking out his Press Pass and pinning it to his lapel.

What have you got there?

JEREMY You'd look naked without one.

SUSAN Oh, yes! Where's mine? I want to look like you.

James joins them. There follows a little charade of mock sympathy.

What about James?

Jeremy and Susan chorus a sympathetic moan.

JEREMY We'll see what we can do.

SUSAN Promise?

JEREMY Promise.

87 Brighton promenade, day

James, Jeremy and Susan walk along the promenade and cross the road towards the Grand Hotel. The Conference Centre is visible and so too are the police and demonstrators. Jeremy has linked arms with Susan. James lags behind a little. Jeremy tells a joke, barely audible above the sound of traffic and the chants of the protestors. Susan giggles as she and Jeremy skip forward to dodge the traffic.

88 Lobby, Grand Hotel, day

The lobby is crowded with delegates, MPs, Press and TV people.

JEREMY There goes my deep throat. Excuse me.

Jeremy darts away. Susan is looking about her.

JAMES Shall we have a drink or something?

SUSAN Oh . . . excuse me. There's Nicholas.

James is left.

89 Hotel balcony, afternoon

Delegates and MPs, and media people, are taking tea on the long balcony of the Grand Hotel. Jeremy is interviewing an MP. James and Susan sit at the same table listening.

JEREMY Then, the theory goes, you'll be back in favour. In line for a real job. Is that right?

MP Well, it's a theory . . . interesting. Oh, excuse me, there's Willy.

The MP makes off.

JEREMY I want to see him too.

Jeremy leaves. James comes and sits closer to Susan.

JAMES We don't seem to get much time to talk.

SUSAN I know. I'm sorry.

An announcement comes through on the hotel's PA.

PA Miss Susan Barrington, Miss Susan Barrington. A phone call for you.

Susan makes a half-hearted apologetic gesture and leaves. As she goes she passes Jeremy who holds a Press Pass for James. He kneels by James's chair and pins the card to his lapel.

JEREMY General Sir James Penfield . . . services during the Norfolk campaign.

90 Conference Centre, late afternoon

The three walk towards the Conference Centre, along the gauntlet of protestors and onlookers. Among them are Carmen and Betty, holding a placard which says 'Women's Peace Camp'. They catch sight of James. Some puzzled recognition. James hurries away from the women and through the doors into the Centre.

91 Press balcony, Conference Centre, day

James, Susan and Jeremy come onto the Press balcony and find their seats while Francis Pym delivers a speech.

PYM It was they who rebuffed aggression, they who struck such a powerful blow for democracy . . .

JAMES (*to Susan*) I managed to book us a table at Wheelers.

PYM I believe this will prove of wider significance even than the event itself. We were seen to be fighting to defend principles which are fundamental to free nations everywhere, and our reputation has been enhanced as a result.

JEREMY (*to Susan*) Francis is in cracking form, don't you think?

92 Bar, early evening

James, Jeremy and Susan. Journalists, delegates etc.

SUSAN (*triumphant, excited*) It was incredible. He came back, made a pompous little bow and said, 'My dear girl you may film me all afternoon if you wish.' *And* he's promised not to talk to the Press.

JEREMY It's because he desires you. The women get all the breaks at these conferences.

SUSAN It's true! I was here last year doing a piece, remember? I was in the bar with all these Northern trade unionists and their sponsored MPs. They were all incredibly fat and beery, huge trousers and braces. And *so* sweet. They all stood round me like children saying '*You*? Working for television? You're just a young thing.' They wouldn't let me buy drinks even when I told them the programme was paying. They kept looking at my pass which was pinned here and saying (*Mock Yorkshire*) 'Oo, can I?'

JEREMY Then one of them was sick all over your new dress.

SUSAN No, he wasn't. He just lowered himself into a bar stool and said . . . (*Yorkshire*) 'Oo I do feel bad. I 'ad three pints of lager and six onion bajees!'

They all laugh.

I've got to go. See you at dinner.

She kisses them both. They watch her go. Their different expressions.

JEREMY Six onion bajees! Great girl. (*Then, confidential.*) Did you shake the mother off?

JAMES Yes, finally.

JEREMY Big mistake, I think. You might have learned a lot.

JAMES (*sudden*) Are you up to something?

Jeremy shrugs innocently and shows his empty hands.

93 Conference Centre, day

James wanders through the Centre in search of Susan. He enters the debating chamber. Michael Heseltine is addressing the Conference. James wanders out to the space below the platform where journalists and photographers are gathered. He goes up the aisles between the seated delegates. No sign of Susan. He leaves the chamber.

HESELTINE . . . left-wing councils employ labour candidates in the paid voluntary sector. We now face a professional left financed at the ratepayer's and tax payer's expense! Just more money is not a solution in itself. As we have given more money to the professional left . . .

94 Lobby, Conference Centre, day

Much later, James crosses the crowded lobby, still in search of Susan.

95 Stairs, Conference Centre, day

James climbs the stairs to the Press balcony. He hears Mrs Thatcher's voice, and from the street below, the chanting of protestors.

THATCHER *(off)*. This is not going to be a speech about the Falklands campaign, although I would be proud to make one. But I want to say just this because it is true for all our people.

96 Press balcony, day

James passes through the doors and finds a seat.

THATCHER The spirit of the South Atlantic was the spirit of
Britain at her best. It has been said that we surprised the
world, that British patriotism was rediscovered in those spring
days. Mr President, it was never really lost!

*James suddenly notices Susan down on the lower floor. She
passes through the doors and is gone. James gets to his feet.*

But it would be no bad thing if the feeling that swept over
the country then were to continue to inspire us. But if there
was any doubt about the determination of the British people . . .

*Jeremy and Susan come through the doors onto the Press
balcony. James stops. They have not seen him. He watches
as they stand together. Clearly a new intimacy has been
established.*

. . . it was removed by men and women who a few months
ago brought a renewed sense of pride and self-respect to our
country.

*Jeremy kisses the nape of Susan's neck. They are not interested
in staying for the speech. James watches stonily as they leave.*

They were for the most part young. Let all of us here, and in
the wider audience outside, pause and reflect . . .

Numbed, James returns to his seat.

. . . on what we who stayed at home owe to those who sailed
and fought and lived and died and won. If this is tomorrow's
generation, then Britain has little to fear in the years to come!

Mix to the last sentence of the Prime Minister's speech.

We will tell the people the truth, and the people will be our judge!

James sits through the standing ovation. The delegates cheer, 'Land of Hope and Glory' is sung. James chews his nails.

97 Conference Centre, day

Hours later. Workmen are dismantling the platforms, taking away props, taking down the Conference backdrop and slogans. In long-shot we see Jeremy making his way between the rows of chairs. James pursues him enraged, shouting. The ad libbed obscenity can barely be heard.

98 Brighton sea front, dusk

James and Jeremy.

James's rage is spent. It has collapsed into bitterness. The two men stop under a street lamp.

JEREMY Susan and I are very old friends, James.

JAMES Fuck off.

JEREMY And you were obviously getting nowhere with her. I was waiting for the right moment to tell you that.

JAMES My God. You even cooked up that Norfolk trip.

JEREMY It might have worked. Really. I would have been

delighted for you if it had. But she wasn't interested. Not my fault.

JAMES You're a piece of shit.

JEREMY I've known Susan for more than fifteen years. James, we're old allies.

At this last word, James looks up. Jeremy walks away.

99 James's flat, day

A few weeks later. We don't see James. We see and hear words pounding onto the page. A fury in the typing. The page is pulled clear. Silence. We stay on the typewriter.

100 BBC Newsroom, day

James is leaving in a hurry. He pulls on a thick overcoat, gathers up some papers, ignores someone who calls after him as he leaves.

101 Langham Place, day

James leaves Broadcasting House and walks towards Oxford Circus.

102 Gold's office, day

Gold stands by his desk as James comes in, pouring two glasses of wine.

GOLD James . . . I can't begin to tell you how pleased we all are. (*He hands James a glass.*) Congratulations, and I really mean it.

JAMES Thank you.

GOLD It's everything we wanted. A very good read. A terrific piece of work. So, here's to you and Suez.

JAMES And to history.

Close in, the glasses touch.

103 Cemetery, day

A group of mourners round a grave. A grey day. A priest reads from the Book of Common Prayer, but his voice is virtually lost to us. We find James's father, hunched in his overcoat, face immobile with grief. Next to him, James, expressionless.

James glances at his watch.

Freeze frame. Optical zoom.

Ends.